Pattern making ~~~~~ ndry practice; a plain statement of the methods of wood pattern making, as practiced in modern pattern shops, with complete instructions for sweep work and notes on foundry practice, together with numerous drawings taken from actual

L H. b. 1854 Hand

Pattern Making
AND
Foundry Practice

A PLAIN STATEMENT OF THE METHODS OF WOOD PATTERN
MAKING, AS PRACTICED IN MODERN PATTERN SHOPS, WITH COM-
PLETE INSTRUCTIONS FOR SWEEP WORK AND NOTES ON FOUNDRY
PRACTICE, TOGETHER WITH NUMEROUS DRAWINGS TAKEN FROM
ACTUAL PATTERNS WHICH HAVE BEEN SELECTED AT RANDOM
BY THE AUTHOR FROM A MODERN PATTERN ROOM WITH A
VIEW TO ILLUSTRATE THE PROCESSES OF THE CRAFT AND THE
INSTRUCTIONS CONTAINED IN THIS WORK.

*NOTE — The majority of the problems in this book have been
solved, the work performed directly under the supervision of the author.*

By

L. H. HAND, M.E.

Illustrated

FREDERICK J. DRAKE & CO.
PUBLISHERS   CHICAGO
1905

PREFACE

My purpose in writing this book will be apparent from its great usefulness, which, I am quite sure, will be conceded by intelligent and thoughtful readers.

For many years I have been employed in railroad and construction shops and have observed that the principles of pattern making were less understood than any other branch of wood work. I have frequently noticed, in railroad shops especially, that the workmen who could "make a pattern" commanded a better position and were in greater demand than those who could not. In large shops from one to a great many pattern makers are regularly employed, and work is systematically arranged; but in the smaller shops it is very important to have a workman in the cabinet or carpenter shop who is competent to make a correct pattern and who may be called upon at any time to perform this duty, thereby being instrumental in saving much money for his employers.

For a term of years I was employed as general foreman of the wood working department of a factory near one of the large cities on Lake Michigan. This factory, from a very modest start, advanced rapidly in wealth and importance, until its employes were numbered by the hundreds. In the beginning the pattern shop was only a branch of, or rather a bench in, the cabinet shop. For about three years the growth of the pattern shop kept pace with the growth of the plant, until eventually it became a department of itself and passed out from under my supervision.

During my term as foreman of the pattern shop, I observed that workmen who were considered pattern makers were entirely ignorant of some of the simplest problems in pattern making, while others were expert in every detail of the business. I also discovered that there was a great scarcity of literature upon the subject of pattern making, and such as was obtainable was not generally read by the members of the trade. Having become much interested in the various problems with which I was confronted from time to time, I consulted frequently with the intelligent and expert members of the craft, until I became thoroughly familiar with the business in all its details and quite skillful in the actual workshop practice of the art. Being ambitious to become a master of the science, I took great pride in working out difficult problems at the lathe and the bench, and by assiduous and persistent application I soon acquired a substantial reputation as a pattern maker.

Not being engaged in active business last winter, I devoted my leisure time to the preparation of this work, feeling assured that it would confer a lasting benefit upon those of my fellow workmen of the craft, who will study the explanations and illustrations which it contains with the same care and earnestness which I have devoted to their elaboration. The subjects treated relate mainly to patterns which came, from time to time, to my bench or which fell under my observation while I was general foreman of the wood working department in the factory.

A wide and varied experience in the employ of railroads and car shops generally, has convinced me that even the professional pattern maker is ignorant of many comparatively simple problems, while to many careful and close wood workmen the simplest rules are unknown. As evidence corroborating this statement, I will cite an instance of the ignorance of a professional pattern maker whom I once knew. This workman cut up about six dollars' worth of lumber and spent two days' time making a large core box. Later on this core box needed some alterations, and another pattern maker, who had been employed subsequently, was called upon to make the changes. He looked the box over and seemed much amused. Then he picked up some large scraps and four strips of wood of the desired length, and in about thirty minutes he made a skeleton box, at a cost of about thirty or forty cents, which answered all purposes, thereby demonstrating the fact that "knowledge is power," and that the serving of a given time in a pattern shop does not always develop proficiency to its highest plane of usefulness.

Should this work be the means of improving the condition or advancing the wages of any of my fellow laborers, I shall be pleased to hear from them, and their letters will be carefully filed away as the tokens of some fellowmen's burdens which have been made a little lighter through my efforts.

THE AUTHOR.

PATTERN MAKING AND FOUNDRY PRACTICE

PRELIMINARY REMARKS

While the catalogues of publishing houses, dealing in scientific works, abound with handbooks published in the interest of the progressive wood worker who desires to learn all he can about the possibilities of wood construction, and while we may find books devoted to the use of the steel square, building construction, superintendence, different rules and methods for estimating and contracting, forms of specifications and contracts, rules for laying out arches in straight and circular walls, different systems of hand railing and stair building, rules and formulas for determining the strength of materials and estimating the natural strains to which such materials are subject, hopper bevels, hip and valley roof framing, groined ceilings, rake mouldings, roof and bridge trusses and their joints and strength, yet it seems that the particular branch of the art of wood working, which pertains to the making of wood patterns for the moulder's use in making cast metal forms of the various kinds, shapes and dimensions required by the numerous and ever-increasing demands of modern construction, has not been given much attention, as very little literature on this subject exists, and that which does is not read to any extent by the craft, the bulk of information on all technical points being, as it were, carried by tradition from foreman to apprentice. In view of this fact, it occurred to me that an exhaustive and comprehensive work on this subject, giving the results of years of practical experience, elucidated by clear and concise instructions and illustrated by drawings, cannot fail to supply an urgent want in the ever-growing complexity of this masterful era of mechanical progress.

This work is destined not only to aid the well trained and skillful artisan by simplifying many difficult and seemingly impossible tasks, but it will become an indispensable source of educational advantage to the inexperienced mechanic and apprentice.

There is absolutely nothing known as to the

origin of the process of casting metal forms from wood patterns. Among the relics of prehistoric man there are weapons, implements and vessels of bronze which, by inevitable inference, we must concede were cast in moulds made by embedding either a pattern of wood or other material in sand or earth. The very discovery of metal, in all probability, owes its origin to the accidental fusing of some kind of ore, and the form of the cavity in the earth in which it has cooled suggested to the mind of primitive man the wonderful process of moulding, which has been so great a factor in the marvelous development of the human race. Patient scientific research has revealed incontrovertible evidence that the art of moulding in earth is one of high antiquity, and this justifies the deduction that pattern making also as a craft, though no doubt struggling through long periods of time in a state of primitive crudity, is of almost equally remote origin, as the conception and necessity of a pattern to construct the mould would most naturally follow the discovery of the fusion of ores into the various forms given to the cooled metal by the accidents of its position in earth or sand.

In the early history of pattern making the art was not separated from ordinary wood working. It was a branch of the millwright or wheelwright trade, and answered all the purposes and wants of that period; but the demands of modern manufacture are so multitudinous and exacting that the highest order of skill has become an imperative necessity in every department of the wood worker's trade.

The wonderful improvement in machinery during the past century has created a demand for forms in casting, so numerous in their endless variety, that the vocation of the modern pattern maker has become a specialized art requiring scientific knowledge highly developed, and coupled with the ability to apply this knowledge practically to the requirements of modern mechanical discovery and invention.

It is therefore of the utmost importance that every mechanic who selects for his vocation in life that of the pattern maker, should thoroughly master all the technical knowledge of the art, not only for his own temporal interests, but for that still higher motive which actuates all zealous workers in every department of human endeavor and who reap as their reward, in addition to

material ... ... of ... ...
that they ... ... the
onward march ... ... progress ... ...
... ... it may be ... ...
... the pattern maker ... ...
... not made ... yet the great population of
... ... a ... ...
to the efficiency of patient research and tireless
industry in the achievement of ... great things.

Nineteen ... ... on arrival he was a
young man who ... from ... ...
great cities and found employment in a large
brass foundry engaged in the manufacture of
valves, ... fittings ... In ... ...
from the time he started ... ... he rose to a
foreman of the pattern shop and ... that
position for years. An that ... ...
a foreman made his own patterns and ... ...
for a grain binder which ... the grain ...
the straw. The binder proved to be a ... ...
... the introduction of the twine ... ...
... the problem in a ... ... manner. The
... large binder concerns who had this ...
... under consideration, became alarmed and
joined the general stampede to the twine binder
causing a loss to the farmer inventor of all ...

labor on the machine. These two instances, however, of rapid success and utter failure, represent the extremes of good and bad fortune rather than the average medium of success which always attends assiduous application and persistent endeavor in the aggregate.

The principal aim of the pattern maker should be to make himself so absolute a master of his work that the solution of all problems with which he may be confronted can be quickly obtained and with the least possible expense. The modern pattern maker should be thoroughly familiar with all the rules for draft shrinkage, etc., and ready to apply them at a moment's notice.

Under the old régime, the millwright hewed the timber, framed his building and made the patterns for boxing, gear wheels, etc. He then set up the machinery, officiating practically as millwright, machinist, pattern maker and carpenter; in fact, he was a veritable mechanical factotum; and yet, although the millwright is credited with the ability to figure out the speed of gears, pulleys, etc., and to set up machinery, he may be totally ignorant of the simplest rules for shrinkage, draft, etc. Hence the importance of specialized labor in the vast number of de-

partments which have been created by the neces-
sities of the gigantic industrial world of modern
times, as better results are obtained and time
and money saved. Living as we do in this age
of high pressure and quick results, it is incum-
bent upon every worker to do his part with as
little expenditure of time, energy and money as
possible, or the procession will pass him by and
he will be consigned to the rear in the ranks of
that great army of those who are unfit to continue the fierce struggle of existence under modern industrial conditions.

The old time buggy maker, who was black-
smith and wheelwright, body maker, trimmer
and painter, was wont to build a few vehicles
like the famed "one hoss shay," but they were
so expensive that only a very few people, excep-
tionally fortunate could afford to own them. In
these days half a dozen smiths make as many
different parts of the gear, while the man who
welds the tires could not in all probability forge
the simplest part of the gear, and the curtain
maker may never see the top of the buggy.
The gear may be made in Grand Rapids, the
shafts in Indianapolis, the body wherever the
least money will buy the largest box, and the

parts assembled in Chicago. Then the finished product is put on the market at a price so low that the barefooted boy in the country can take his grist to mill in a buggy. In fact, buggies have become so cheap that, driving along almost any country road, one will often pass a buggy wreck piled up in a fence corner or in a side ditch. These wrecked vehicles are not entirely worn out, but the price of a new buggy is so low that it is cheaper to buy one than to incur the expense of repairs upon the old one.

A thorough division of labor, while it forces a mechanic to become, as it were, a cog in the wheel of some great machine, which grinds the same round from day to day and month to month, also cheapens the product of every mechanic's labor, so that now people of small means are not denied the products of mill, loom and factory, which half a century ago were only obtainable by the very rich. With the ever-increasing demand for cheaper production, pattern making is destined to become more and more a trade to be desired. The destruction of the forests and the presence of the iron mountain in Missouri are two fixed facts, indicating where we will be forced in the near future to

seek our raw material which heretofore the great
forests have supplied. With the disappearance of
the timber, iron is slowly and almost imper-
ceptibly but surely taking its place. I have
heard old men bewail the condition of the country when the supply of rail timber becomes exhausted, and yet what farmer would split the
rails now if he were given free of cost the timber? The wooden fence post is rapidly making
way for cast iron or a block of concrete with a
rolled sheet iron standard. The wooden railroad
bridge has almost disappeared, and even country
road bridges are now nearly all built of iron.
Wooden buildings now only exist because the
forests have not entirely disappeared, and wood
in its first cost is yet cheaper than other and
better material for construction. The railroad
cross tie is yet a perplexing problem; nevertheless,
when the timber for its manufacture is entirely
exhausted, necessity will give birth to some
ingenious device or substitute in iron, glass, concrete or paper, which will supersede the present
wooden cross tie, and will in all probability prove
so far superior to it that those of a generation or
so to come will contemplate with amusement the
primitive methods employed by their fathers in

the construction of roadbed, just as we of this generation look with jocose good nature upon the old wooden plow of our ancestors.

It should not be inferred that any arbitrary set of rules can be devised governing the making of every description of pattern which the workman may be called upon to produce. The nearest approach to an unerring guide, covering the widest range of the subject, is the classification of certain forms of patterns with drawings illustrating each class, with concise and lucid explanations by which the well-informed and intelligent mechanic can work out problems in whatever class they may appear. This is what the author has done in this work, and in a manner to insure the certain accomplishment of his purpose, and yet the hope is nowhere excited throughout this work, either by direct statement or implication, that any self-educational facilities afforded by the study of this work will supply the deficiency of natural mechanical talent which must primarily be possessed by any person who may hope to excel in any department of mechanical science.

In a factory which employed over one hundred carpenters and cabinetmakers, I do not think there were more than three or four who could or ever did turn anything on the wood lathe, and whenever many of the others attempted to do so a complete failure was the result, notwithstanding the most explicit verbal instructions as to the holding of the tools and the practical demonstration by the instructor taking the tools himself and performing the operation for the students.

In the preparation of this work it has been my aim to simplify and present all problems in a light so clear that the principles at least will be thoroughly understood by any reader of ordinary intelligence; but the practical and successful application of the principles expounded will depend wholly upon the innate ability and careful execution of the operator. Even with native talent of the highest order, rough and careless work will not promote success nor obtain for the workman any creditable reputation.

The work of a pattern maker is clean and pleasant, but requires a very high grade of skill to properly execute, even under the direction of a skillful foreman. The cutting tools should be the very best that the market affords, with edges smooth and keen at all times. To the foreman of the shop every new job is "another problem to solve." There is no precedent for many jobs—no beaten path to follow. Often after a job is completed a better way has been discovered, by which the job could have been done to greater advantage. There have been instances of capable pattern makers widely differing in their views of how certain patterns should be made; each one maintaining vehemently that his method was the only right and proper one.

FOUNDRY PRACTICE

Before entering into the details of pattern making, let us first consider the customary way of making castings; for if we are ignorant of the manner in which the moulder obtains the proper cavity in the sand by the use of the wood pattern, it would be impossible to make the pattern to the best advantage. I say this advisedly, and I believe that a first-class moulder can take nearly any object for a pattern and get it out of the sand, leaving the mould perfect, and make a successful casting. It has been authentically related of a certain moulder that he could mould the pronged horns of an antlered buck from the natural pattern as it grew on the animal's head. I remember an instance of a farmer who brought to a small foundry the fire bowl of a heating stove, which was broken in seven pieces. A new bowl was moulded from the pieces, a feat of moulding which suggests a strong argument to the pattern maker and which should convince him that a knowledge of foundry practice is a most powerful auxiliary to his trade, enabling him always to make his patterns.

Castings are usually made in a flask. This is composed of two or more rough boxes, so constructed, by the use of dowels or other devices, as to retain their relative positions at all times when in use. This is absolutely necessary, as otherwise the casting would be one-sided or would show a jog at the joint or parting.

When more than two boxes are used, this flask is called a compound flask. Usually only two boxes are used, and this arrangement is called a two-part flask. The upper box is called the cope, and the lower box the drag. The heaviest portions of a casting are usually left in the drag, which naturally retains its shape, thereby minimizing the risk of agitating the sand, whereas the cope has to be lifted and moved around, which has a great tendency to disturb the sand in it and break and destroy the mould. To overcome this danger, it is customary to put rods or wooden bars, or both, across the cope, through the sand, wherever they can be placed without interfering with the pattern. Then bars and rods hold the sand in shape so that they can be lifted to remove the pattern and replaced to make the finished mould. Where it is possible to do so, it is best to make a parting in the wooden pattern at the point where the sand in the cope and drag divide on a straight line. This done, that part of the pattern which is to be left in the drag is placed on a flat board or bench, with the parting down. The drag is placed in an inverted position on the same board or bench and "rammed up"; that is to say, filled and tamped solidly with moulding sand. The drag is then placed right side up on the foundry floor and the upper part of the pattern is put on. A parting is then made with fine dry parting sand and the cope is secured in place and rammed up. Holes are then made down through the cope to the pattern, for the purpose of pouring the metal into the mould and also to allow the air to escape. The flask is then taken apart and the wooden pattern removed, leaving the two halves of the mould, which are then placed in their proper positions, making a complete and finished mould. In ordinary work a board, which is the size of the flask and is called a "follow board," is used for parting. For some special work, a special follow board is used, as in cases when the parting would describe a

curve. In other cases a follow board is made
for a single piece pattern, like the hand wheel
for a car break, by bedding the pattern one-half
its depth in plaster of Paris, thus bringing the
parting to the center of the pattern without any
parting in the wooden pattern and without the
use of the trowel. All these things are done for
convenience to the moulder, so that he can make
time in getting out his work.

The first thing to be considered in looking at
a pattern is how it will best draw out of the
sand. Every complicated form of casting presents a partially new problem to the pattern
maker. If a piece will readily draw out of the
sand except one or more small projections, they
can sometimes be left on a dovetail slide, which
will allow the pattern to be drawn, leaving a
part in the sand to be removed later on; or if it
be a cavity, it must be cored out.

In preparing this work I have begun with the
simplest forms and kinds of patterns, progressing
gradually through the more difficult features of
the work, and for illustrations I have used prin-
cipally patterns which may be found in duplicate
in the pattern loft of the Hicks Locomotive and
Car Works, near Chicago. These patterns have

been made by different pattern makers and have been selected with a view to properly illustrate ideas and demonstrate such peculiarities of con- structions as are treated in this work.

The very simplest form of pattern is repre- sented by the cast iron washer, Fig. 1. This pattern, being straight on one side, lies entirely below the parting and is consequently entirely in the drag. When a great many pieces of any article of this class are required, it is customary to make what is called a "gated pat- tern," which consists of a

Fig 1
Cross section through a cast washer

number of patterns made exactly alike and fastened together with small strips let into the straight side, level with its face. Then small strips lying on the follow board leave little grooves in the sand which allow the molten metal to pass freely into all the moulds, which are easily broken apart when the metal cools. This manner of moulding this kind of pattern is similar to that previously described, except that the cope is simply placed on the drag and filled with sand, as there is no part of the pattern

projecting up into it. A better understanding of
this may be derived by a study of A-1, Fig 2,
which shows a cross-section through the drag,
the pattern, the follow board and the sand
rammed up. Fig. 2 shows the cross-section of
the entire box and its contents ready to be inverted and placed on the foundry floor, when the
follow board is removed and the cope secured in

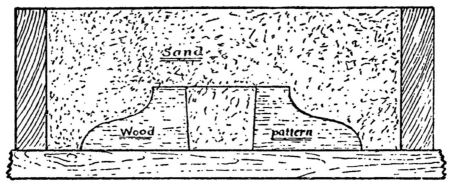

Fig 2
Cross section through pattern in the sand

place and filled up as previously described. See
Fig. 3, which shows a cross-section through the
mould finished and ready to receive the moulten
metal.[1]

The next form to be considered is of a class
which, while being all in one piece, is of such a

---

[1] It is deemed more expedient to make most of the
illustrations in this work in cross section, as a clearer
understanding of the subject is generally derived from
that character of design.

shape as to render the moulding of the casting more convenient when it is entirely up in the cope. If executed otherwise, the sand in the

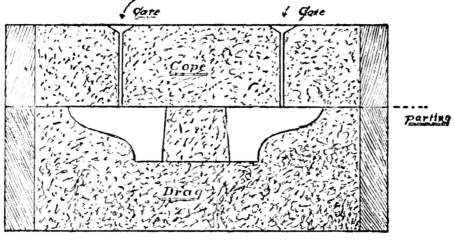

Fig 3
Cross section through finished mould

cope would make it heavy and clumsy and very difficult to handle and the cope would have a tendency to drop off and ruin the mould.[1] In

---

[1] It should be borne in mind that the manner of making the mould depends entirely upon the nature of the work and the purpose for which it is to be used.

Thus it will be found that all, or nearly all, stove castings are made in a manner exactly the reverse from that which is employed in the moulding of ordinary castings. The hollow or concave parts are usually made down in the drag, and the sand in the cope is strengthened by cross bars of wood fitted in such a manner as to come as near the metal as is practicable, and these bars are driven full of nails or made with other projections in order to prevent the sand falling out. By this means a smooth casting on the outer surface is obtained, as the metal, being heavier than the dross or other foreign substances,

this case the pattern, which is assumed to be hollow or of cup shape (see Fig. 4), should be placed on the follow board with the cup or hollow downward. Over this should be placed that part of the flask which is to be used for the cope, and it should then be rammed up in the

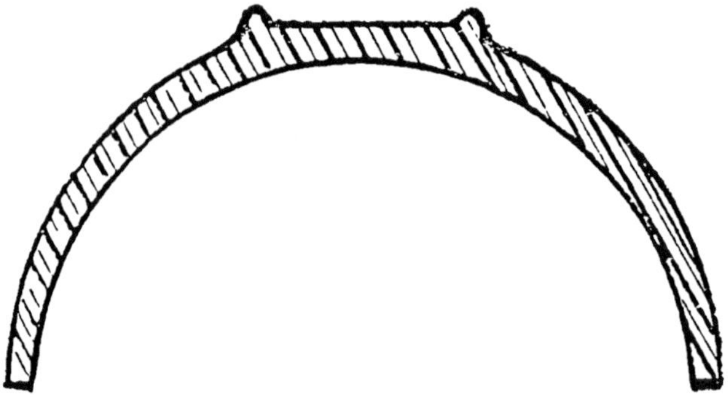

Fig 4

Cross section through cup

settles to the bottom of the mould and shows a perfectly smooth surface, while the imperfections float to the top or inside of the sheet. In small shops where repair work is done, the ingenuity of the flask maker is often taxed to devise means for making flasks perform work for which they were not intended, for the reason that in cases where only one piece of casting is required, the cost of making a special flask would be more than the value of the casting. In factories such as stove works, etc., where a great number of similar pieces are required, many flasks are made for particular pieces, such for instance as oven doors, fire-backs, etc. In these cases the flasks are specially designed with a view to performing the work with the least possible amount of labor by the moulder. There are a great many devices for holding the flasks in position, and some very ingenious patented hinges, clamps, etc.; but most moulders use a square-jawed dog or clamp, which is a fraction longer than the height of the flask

usual manner, after which the proper vents to receive the moulten metal should be made.[1]

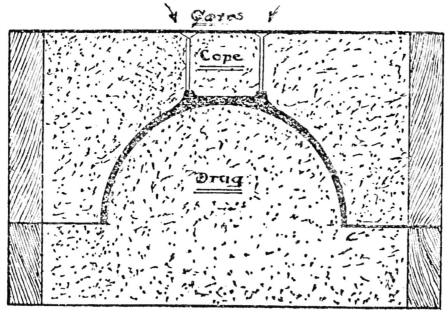

Fig 5
Cross section through mould

The cope should then be turned over, the follow board removed and the drag placed in position and rammed up.   Then the flask (cope and

---

(cope and drag).   This clamp is slipped on the flask and then crowded into a slightly diagonal position with a short bar or chisel, used as a pry, and which holds the boxes firmly together.   For small work the flask is hinged together on one side with an iron hinge so designed as to be readily slipped apart.

[1] The vents or holes down through the cope for pouring the metal, are called gates, and are made by placing tapered pins or wedges of proper size in the cope and touching the wood pattern.   These, being withdrawn, leave the desired gates or ways for the molten metal to pass into the mould in the sand.

drag) should again be turned over, taken apart
and the wood pattern removed, leaving the finished mould as shown in cross-section, Fig. 5.
In many instances it is customary to part the
sand entirely by the use of the moulder's trowel,
especially where the pattern is of some simple
form, or where only a few pieces are required,
as, for example, the small connecting rod shown
in Fig. 6. In this case a flask is filled with sand
and smoothed off, after which the pattern or

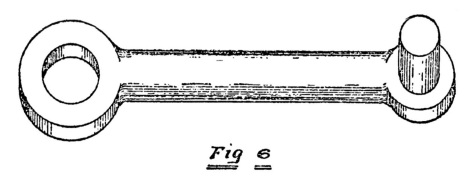

Fig 6

patterns are pushed down into the sand about
half of their depth, or to such a point as will
most readily permit their withdrawal from either
way. The moulder then smoothes the sand
down and packs it thoroughly around the pattern with his trowel. Then a parting is made
with dry sand and the cope is placed in position
and rammed up as previously described. See
Fig. 7, which shows a cross-section through the
same pattern in the sand. Many other forms of

castings are parted in this manner where the
parting, instead of being on a plane with the
parting in the flask, is curved or has sudden
crooks and offsets. In such cases the sand is
packed in the drag to conform as nearly as possible to the crooks in the parting. The pattern
is then placed in position and bedded firmly in
the sand. The moulder then packs and trowels
down the sand around the pattern until a perfect

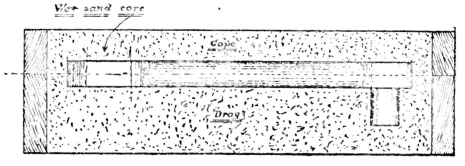

Fig 7

Sectional view of mould for Fig 6 Showing pattern in sand

parting is made, sometimes cutting deep cavities
around portions which otherwise would tear
out the sand in drawing the pattern. In this
manner an expert moulder will get out forms
which at first glance look to be impossible. But
primarily it is the duty of the pattern maker so to
construct his patterns as to reduce to a minimum
of intricacy all of these difficult problems with
which the moulder may be confronted. As an
instance of the value of a correctly-made pattern

as an initial desideratum, see Fig. 7a, which illustrates a small fire extinguisher top and which, at a cursory glance, appears very difficult, but which in reality is readily drawn out of the sand. This is a cup-shaped brass casting with round, projecting handles serving to screw and unscrew it. A cross-section of this is shown in the sand in Fig. 7a. The heavy lines show

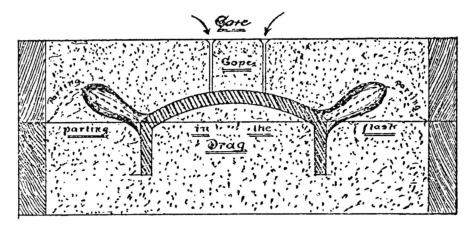

Fig 7 a
Cross section through fire extinguisher top & mould

the parting in the flask and the dotted lines show the parting in the sand.

It is of the greatest importance that a pattern should have draft; that is to say, it must be of such a shape that it will begin to loosen from the sand the moment a move is made to draw it out. To facilitate a ready loosening and successful withdrawal from the sand, all pattern work should be slightly out of square or slightly beveled; i.e., it should be a trifle smaller at the portions which are embedded the deepest in the sand. Then again, the moulder often raps some patterns very heavily to get them out. That is to say, a pointed iron, which is driven into the wood pattern for the purpose, is smartly struck in all directions, causing the mould to become larger than the pattern. Some patterns are so shaped that they cannot be drawn out of the sand, as they may be hollow and of irregular form, or contain cavities or projecting parts which would tear out or loosen the sand. In all such cases it becomes necessary to use cores, to prepare which boxes or moulds are made of the proper shape. Into these boxes or moulds a preparation of sand with flour and molasses is packed, and the forms or cores so made are baked in an oven. After being thoroughly baked, these cores become firm enough to stand handling and will support their own weight across a considerable space. For certain purposes cores are sometimes made by substituting linseed oil, rosin, etc., for flour and molasses, and these are considered superior, as they make a smoother and stronger casting.

In some instances the required cavity in the casting will be of such a form, or may be complicated in such a manner, as to render it very difficult to mould the desired core in a single box, and therefore in many instances two or more cores are made and glued together. The cores for some of the parts of improved pneumatic tools in use in modern boiler shops have been made up of from twenty to thirty pieces where the desired cavity was so complicated as to be impossible of construction in a single core box. It is also frequently desirable to use cores on work which could be drawn in the ordinary manner, and this is when the casting is hollow and thin enough to spring easily. In all cases where cores are used, the pattern, instead of being the shape of the desired casting alone, should have certain projections, termed "core prints," added to it. These core prints leave their impression in the sand, thus forming a cavity to hold the projecting ends of the core. In such cases it is necessary that the pattern maker should construct his core boxes in such a manner as to produce a core of the exact shape required by the cavity in the casting, together with such projecting parts as will exactly fill the cavities in the sand left by the core prints on the pattern. To illustrate this idea, a stake pocket, such as may be seen on the sides of a gondola flat or coal car, has been selected, the pocket itself being of the form shown in Fig. 8. This will readily draw out of the sand and it is frequently cast in this manner; but on account of

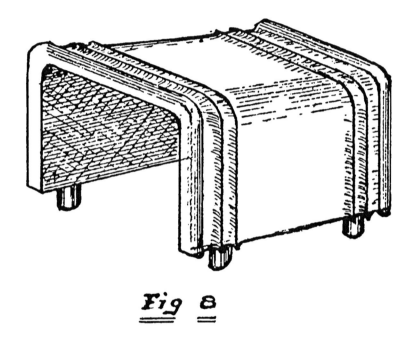

Fig 8

its thinness it is more apt to spring out of shape than if it were cast with a core, as shown in Fig. 9.

Patterns are painted in such a way as to show which portions are iron, and the core prints are left white or painted of a light color. Usually colored shellac is used for the black portions and uncolored for the core prints. By this means the moulder can tell at a glance the moment he takes up the pattern just how to make the casting. Recently, through the carelessness or ignorance of a pattern maker, over two hundred pounds of cast fittings in the Frisco R. R. shops at Cape Girardeau, Mo., were cast solid instead of hollow, because of the entire piece having been painted black, when the core print should have

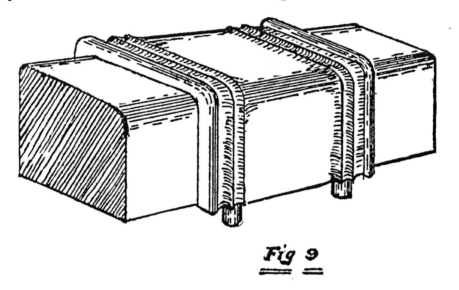

Fig 9

been left light.   In moulding patterns of the class shown in Figs. 9 and 10, the process is much the same as has already been described.   The lugs "a" "a", Fig. 10, are made removable, and when removed the pattern, Fig. 9, is laid flat on the follow board.   The drag is then placed in position and rammed up; then it is turned over and the lugs "a" and "a" inserted, the cope secured in its proper position, the parting made and the cope rammed up, as heretofore described. The flask is then separated and the wood pattern, Fig. 9, is removed and in its place the core is laid, making the complete mould, as shown in Fig. 10.

Small patterns are often gated together, as previously mentioned, or a flask is leveled off and a quantity of them stuck around here and there,

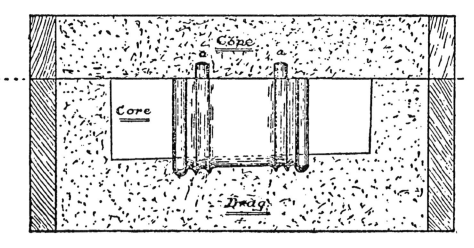

Fig 10

Sectional view of mould for Fig's 8 & 9 showing pattern in sand

while in other cases the pattern will be almost too large to be put in a flask at all. In such cases it is customary to dig a pit in the floor of the foundry to answer for the drag, and in the case of large castings, such as flywheels, engine beds, etc., the pattern itself is so heavy that it can be handled only by the use of a power hoist or crane.

PATTERN SHOP PRACTICE

It is customary in pattern shops to furnish the pattern maker with a mechanical drawing or blue print of the part to be made. This is very important, in fact almost an indispensable part of the work, and yet often this drawing falls far short as a reliable guide to the pattern maker; for while it may indicate clearly enough the style of casting desired, it may contain no directions or suggestions which will govern or assist the pattern maker in the construction of the pattern. Although the office drawing may be a perfect representation of the casting itself, the pattern maker's drawing should show not only the casting, but also the cores, core prints, etc., etc., and where practicable the pattern maker's drawing should be full size, in order that the dimensions may be taken directly from the drawing with the dividers. Some shops may only employ a rough sketch with figured dimensions, and this is especially true of large repair shops, the foremen of which will send a man fifty or a hundred miles down the road to repair engines or cars which have become temporarily disabled. This man will frequently find a cracked or worn out casting or a burned out set of grate bars, in which event the number and date of the engine will be noted and every effort will be made to secure a correct description of the broken part in order that the blue prints of the engine may be consulted and the part located exactly. It often occurs, however, that the blue prints of a damaged engine have been mislaid; consequently the pattern maker is instructed to make, say, a gate bar for the engine and have it ready for the engine immediately upon its arrival at the shop. Having failed to find the blue prints of the engine, the foreman, as a last resource, carries to the pattern shop a memorandum sketch taken from the notebook of the mechanic who had been sent to repair the engine, and from this crude drawing (see Fig. 00) the pattern maker is required, at very short notice, to make a pattern which will give satisfactory results. Any old employe of a railroad shop will recognize this character of drawing (Fig. 00). It is apparent, therefore, that the pattern maker should understand mechanical drawing, at least to an extent sufficient to enable him to make full size working drawings of any piece of pattern work which he contemplates producing.

Drawing is the art of representing objects on a plain surface by the use of lines and shadows. Mechanical drawings are further illustrated and explained by the use of dotted lines, figures, letters, etc. For certain purposes mechanical drawings are sometimes made in perspective; but for pattern shop uses perspective effect is never employed. Two or more views of any object

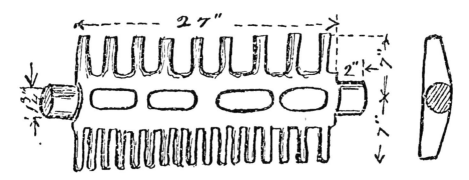

Fig. 00

treated should be given in a mechanical drawing. The art of drawing in a very high state of practical usefulness is now taught by several correspondence schools, and it may be readily acquired by any ambitious person.

Ordinary drawings for most patterns may be made with a lead pencil, a pair of dividers with a pencil point, a pair of beam compasses or trammel points and a steel square. Many old pattern makers use no other tools and make their drawings on the surface of a smooth plank, which only needs planing off to be ready for the next job. A much better way, however, for an important job is to make the drawing on heavy manila paper, which can be filed away for future reference. Where paper drawings are to be used

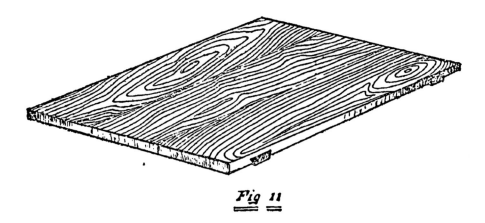

Fig 11

it will be found very convenient to have a few regular drawing instruments. The drawing board should be of any convenient size and made of well-seasoned, clear, soft pine, perfectly straight and square, with hardwood cleats driven snugly into dovetail gains or grooves across the back of the board, as shown in Fig. 11. The T-square is used for drawing parallel lines, either way, across the board, and is made

of any hard, straight-grained wood. Pear wood
is excellent for this purpose; mahogany, cherry
and maple also being used. A most excellent
T-square is made for the trade with a trans-
parent celluloid edge. A proper T-square for
pattern shop use should have a blade at least

Fig 12

three feet long, $3' \times 2\frac{1}{2}'' \times \frac{3}{16}''$, and slightly
beveled toward the edges, with a head $2\frac{1}{2}'' \times \frac{1}{2}''$
fastened securely at right angles to the blade.
The most approved form of joint for a T-square
is shown at *a b*, Fig. 13. A tapered dovetailed
wedge is glued to the blade of the square with

Fig 13

the grain of the parts running at right angles to
each other. A corresponding notch or mortise is
made across the head of the square, which allows
the blade to be taken out of the head and trued
up. The joint can be better secured by the use
of a few round-head screws, if desired. The

set squares or angles are used to draw parallel
lines, at right angles to the blade of the
T-square; or to draw such angles as appear in
the corner of the set squares (see Fig. 14). The
first of these set squares contains an angle of 45°
in two corners and an angle of 90° or a right
angle in the other. This is used to lay out octa-
gons, or to bisect the right angle, producing a

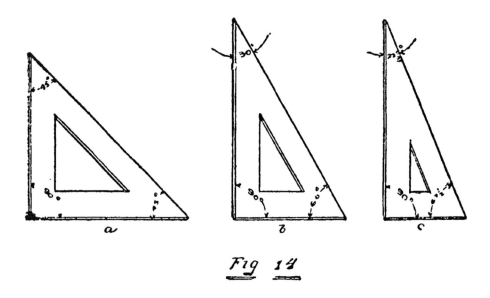

Fig 14

miter joint. The second one contains angles of
30°, 60° and 90°. This square is employed to
lay off the hexagon, or bisect the angles of the
hexagon in order to obtain the hexagon miter.
The third one contains angles of $22\frac{1}{2}°$, $67\frac{1}{2}°$ and
90°, and is used to bisect the angles of the
octagon, obtaining the octagon miter (see a b c,
Fig. 14). Some few extra large wooden set

squares are yet in use for certain purposes; but for general use the modern celluloid or amberoid instruments are so far superior, on account of their transparency, that the wooden ones have fallen into disuse.

A set of mathematical instruments may be bought for from $2.00 to $25.00 or more, according to the fancy of the purchaser. The very

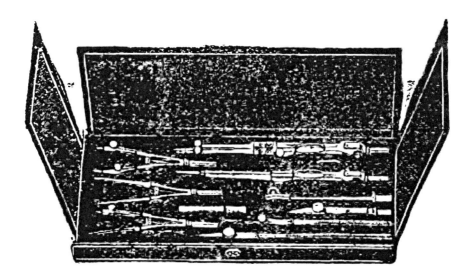

Fig 15

cheap ones are not desirable, and in buying instruments or tools it is always advisable to provide the very best that one's means will permit. An indifferent mechanic can never do good work with inferior tools and a good one will not use them when he can possibly avoid it. The set shown in Fig. 15 has fairly good points and will answer very well for persons of limited means. A set of this kind retails for about $6.00 and will answer every purpose for the class of drawings required in the pattern shop.

In making up the working drawings for shop use it is preferable to trace the outlines faintly with a sharp, hard lead pencil. After this has been done the drawing can be brought out with ink or a soft, black lead pencil. When the drawing has been plainly brought out, some draftsmen give the cores or core prints a yellow tint and darken the parts which are to be metal. This not only improves the appearance of the drawing, but has additional advantages, especially if some workman other than the draftsman is to work from the drawing, in which event the coloring of the drawing obviates the risk of any misconception of what the finished pattern is to be, thereby preventing what might otherwise result in awkward mistakes. Mechanical drawing, being a scientific subject in itself and one which for an elaborate elucidation would involve a voluminous treatise, can only be cursorily referred to in a book of this nature, and it must therefore be assumed that the reader is sufficiently familiar with the principles and practice of mechanical drawing to readily understand the instructions pertaining to the subject-matter of this work.

The pattern shop should always contain sufficient space to provide for the free and comfortable execution of its greatest volume of production and should be arranged with a view to afford ample room for the advantageous distribution and location of machinery, benches, trestles, clamps, tools, etc. The light should be as nearly perfect as it is possible to obtain and preferably derived through skylights which direct the rays vertically upon the work, thereby escaping the shadows thrown upon it by light which strikes it horizontally from the side. The room should be so arranged that a proper temperature can be maintained in winter to insure the successful gluing of work, as cold destroys the adhesive quality of glue and is detrimental to good work in many ways. The work bench is usually made of three-inch plank, in order to keep the top true. The vise should be of modern construction, capable of being used either as a high or low vise, and should be equipped with an adjustable jaw for tapered work, and so arranged as to hold the work firmly without bruising it. The shop should be equipped with a band saw or at least a jig saw, a pattern lathe and suitable clamps for gluing up material. In large shops a rip saw and wood worker will be found very useful. The highest grade of glued work, such as piano and organ cases, sleeping car bunks and fine furniture generally, is made by using hot glue applied to wood which has been heated to receive it; the work being done in a room heated for the purpose. Work glued up in this manner is very strong and better for many purposes than solid timber; but unless special arrangements have been made for this work, ordinary glue is liable to become chilled and lose its strength. There are several preparations of liquid glue which are valuable substitutes in many classes of work where conditions are not favorable to the use of hot glue. These liquid glues, being very slow to set, allow plenty of time to work over a piece where the assembling of the parts is tedious, and the result is far better than that which is obtained by clamping hot glue between two cold surfaces, the effect of which is to convert the glue into a jelly, with little or no adhesive qualities. The workman, however, will have to decide for himself which kind of glue is best suited to the specific conditions of the shop in which he is employed. In shops where the general conditions for gluing are bad, liquid glue promises the best results, when nails, screws or wood dowel pins are used to add such strength to the parts as the nature of the work may demand.

TOOLS

It is highly impracticable to attempt the enumeration of any exhaustive list of tools for pattern making, as the field covers such a wide range of work that unless it were limited to some certain branch of the trade, it would tax the ingenuity of the most resourceful inventor to conceive of such a tool that the wood worker might not at some time meet with a situation requiring its use. To the workman engaged entirely in the making of stove castings, his carving tools are the most important of his kit; while if his work were confined to the making of patterns for heavy machinery, the need of carving tools might never be felt. The making of wood patterns, while the principles involved are much the same in all cases, covers the widest range of work of any branch of the wood worker's art and embraces castings from the size of door keys and window latches to the ponderous parts of the giant engines which supply the water to great cities, turn the wheels of mammoth factories and propel the iron-ribbed reindeers of the

49

sea, hurling them plunging through the green surges of the sea. Most pattern makers carry a very complete assortment of cabinet maker's tools, including their lathe tools or turning chisels, gouges, etc., and also a set of long straight gouges, called pattern maker's gouges, with a set of carving tools for some classes of work. The special tools for pattern making, independent of those in general use, are shown from Fig. 16 to Fig. 22.

Fig. 16 represents the pattern maker's gouge, which is made in all sizes from $\frac{1}{4}$ to 2 inches. This tool is used for making core boxes and for paring out all kinds of convex surfaces. It is indispensable to the pattern maker. Fig. 17 represents the turning gouge, about three sizes of which are usually considered sufficient for all practical purposes. This tool is used for roughing out work in the lathe, and for turning and finishing the concave portions of the work.

Fig. 18 represents a paring tool, of which not more than two sizes are usually needed. This tool is used to finish the work in the lathe after it has been roughly formed by the gouge. The flat chisel, Fig. 19, is used for turning beads, ovals, etc., and for sizing particular work as

indicated by the calipers.   In such cases it is
used much in the same manner as a scraper.

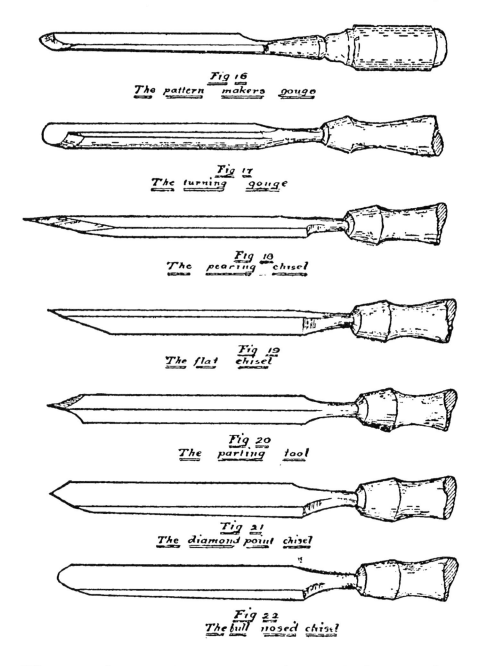

Fig 16
The pattern makers gouge

Fig 17
The turning gouge

Fig 18
The pearing chisel

Fig 19
The flat chisel

Fig 20
The parting tool

Fig 21
The diamond point chisel

Fig 22
The bull nosed chisel

The parting tool, Fig. 20, is used for cutting
deep grooves and for cutting off work in the
lathe.   The diamond point, Fig. 21, and the

bull-nosed chisel, Fig. 22, are used for turning both the outside and inside surfaces of hollow patterns, such as the piece shown in cross-section in Fig. 23.

Figs. 15, 16 and 17 can be procured at hard-

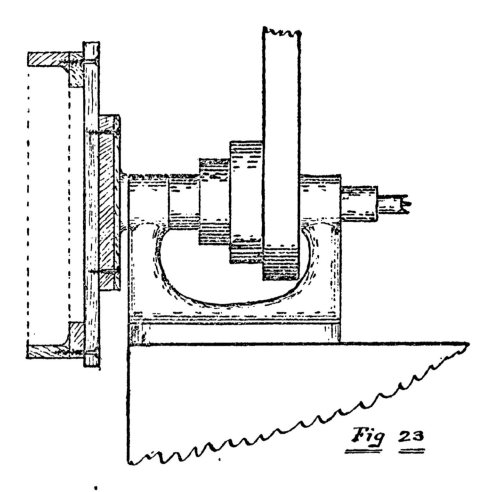

Fig 23

ware stores generally. The rest can be had from large supply houses, or from dealers in tool specialties, or they can be made by a first-class smith. In addition to the tools heretofore mentioned, the pattern maker will sometimes find it convenient to have special tools of a peculiar design for some special work.

The shrinkage rule is a measure designed especially for pattern making, and is intended to make the proper allowance for the contraction of metal in cooling. However, it is not possible to accurately figure the contraction or shrinkage of metal, as a thick casting will shrink more than a thin one. Some shapes shrink more than others or more in some parts of the same piece than in other parts. A large cylinder, if cast on end, will shrink more at the bottom than at the top. Castings are calculated to shrink from one-tenth to one-eighth of an inch to the foot; but, as nearly all machine castings are either turned or planed to an accurate size, the determination of the exact amount of shrinkage is in a great measure immaterial. Then again, in cases where the moulder raps the pattern heavily, in order to withdraw it from the sand, the casting will show but little if any shrinkage.

The lathe is perhaps the most important of all the pattern maker's tools. A lathe suitable for ordinary pattern work should have a swing of at least twelve inches over the bed and it should be so arranged as to allow a face plate for work of large size to be swung off over the end of the bed, as shown in cross-section in Fig. 23. A heavy cast iron tripod of sufficient weight to remain steady when in use, is employed to hold the rest for this lathe.

The art of wood turning has by tradition always been and is at the present time classified as a trade to itself, properly appertaining to the cabinet shop and planing mill; for the art, when applied to pattern making, differs so materially from that of ordinary cabinet and planing mill work, that it cannot be considered in the same category.

The wood turner, working by gauges or marks on the lathe rest representing his measurements, depends almost entirely upon the accuracy of his eye and skill of his hand to obtain the required form and size of the piece; as the compensation for such work is often determined by a fixed rate per thousand pieces, the operator soon acquires a peculiar sleight for getting out a great quantity of material in a given length of time, which, if displayed in regular rows, presents an appearance sufficiently uniform to answer all the purposes for which the finished work is intended, although it could not stand the test of rule and calipers.

The pattern maker, on the contrary, works from a drawing of some part of a machine or other device, showing the figured dimensions of all its parts. Every figure bears an important relation to the finished work and each part is required to correspond with mathematical precision to some other part already completed or in process of completion in another department of the same factory, or mayhap in some distant city. The loss of only the sixteenth of an inch of material in any part may mean the loss of the entire piece. Hence the paramount necessity that the maker should exercise the most scrupulous care during the process of work, stopping frequently as he proceeds to test his accuracy with rule or calipers or both, for only painstaking vigilance will assure to even the most adroit mechanic a perfect duplicate in its minutest detail of the part represented in the drawing. Manifestly, then, the art of the wood turner consists in turning out great quantities of pieces which bear to one another sufficient resemblance to answer the purposes for which they are designed, whilst the science of lathe turning, for pattern making, lies wholly in the accuracy and perfection, and not in the volume of work performed.

In operating the pattern lathe to turn out hollow forms it is customary to fasten discs of wood to the iron face plates of the lathe with heavy wooden screws. The work to be turned is then secured to the face of these discs with other wooden screws passing through the wooden discs into the back of the piece to be turned. See Fig. 23. When a pattern is to be screwed on the face plate, these wooden discs are marked with the point of the turning tool at the outside or inside of the piece, and it can then be turned over and fastened true to center.

To formulate any set of rules which will apply to the production of all kinds of patterns or to the solution of every problem in pattern making which may arise would involve a degree of knowledge and a gift of prophetic vision which cannot be expected to fall to the lot of any observer, however patient may have been his research or broad his experience; therefore, in the treatment of this work, I have availed myself only of such forms of patterns as have been successfully made under my own supervision and observation; using these forms as object lessons to illustrate the subject and impart to the student a practical knowledge of the essential principles of pattern making, in order that he may be well prepared—assuming, of course, the possession of natural talent—to grapple with every new and perplexing problem with which the interminable intricacies of the craft may confront him in any hour of his career. And incidentally I have introduced into this work a few problems submitted to me by workmen familiar with foundry work in all its details, and whilst I have not seen these problems demonstrated by actual practice, my certainty as to the correctness of their illustrations enables me to present them to the reader with the utmost confidence in their practical value.

MAKING THE PATTERN

Many patterns are of the simplest form and require only a single piece of stuff, turned or carved into a proper shape, finished with shellac and having proper draft and shrinkage. These simple patterns are usually given to the apprentice boys to make; for instance, the pattern of a cast washer, such as is represented by Fig. 1.

Assuming this washer to be for a $1\frac{1}{2}$-inch rod, the diameter of the stock would be about 7 inches and the thickness $1\frac{3}{8}$ inches. To make this pattern, a disc is cut out of wood $7\frac{1}{4} \times 1\frac{1}{2}$ inches, one side is made true and straight and it is then secured in the center of the face plate. The pattern is then faced off with the diamond points and the center located with a pair of dividers as the piece runs in the lathe. Next a line is laid off for the center hole, a line for the edge of the O. G. and a line for the outside. Now the operator cuts straight into the face plate on the outside line and with a very small gouge, turned sideways, roughs out the O. G., taking care that it does not jump back and tear up the work.

When the operator is not sufficiently expert with the gouge to turn the O. G. it can be scraped to shape with the bull-nosed chisel. Next the hole is cut out with a small, stiff, flat chisel, leaving plenty of draft. When the pattern is turned it must be sandpapered to a polish, taking extra care that the hole is left smooth. Next shellac of any desired color is applied, and when it begins to set it is polished, while still revolving, with an old cloth and a few drops of linseed oil.

Fig. 6 represents the piece sawed out as near to shape as possible and then carved or whittled and finished with sandpaper and shellac.

Passing on to another class of patterns, the stake pocket affords an apt illustration. This piece is easily cast from a form as shown in Fig. 3. It has sometimes occurred that an old stake pocket has been picked up in the yard, smoothed off a little, the sand holes puttied up and the piece shellacked and used for a pattern for other pockets. This method, however, was only resorted to when it was necessary to get cars ready for service on very short notice. The usual custom and the proper method is to cast this pattern with a core. The procedure for this is as follows: First the working drawing (see

Fig. 24, *a* and *b*) should be made up full size by the shrinkage rule. Next there should be laid out a pattern on a thin veneer of the cross sec-

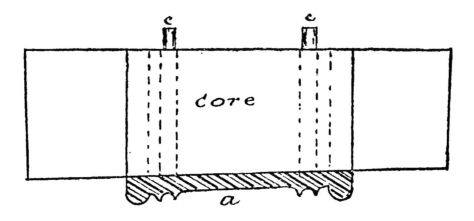

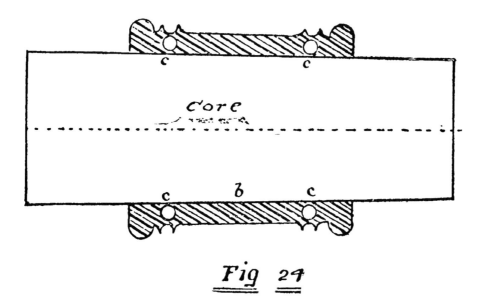

Fig 24

tion through the metal as it appears in the full-size working drawing, and the pattern cut out with a sharp knife. Then this pattern should be plainly marked with a pencil on both ends of a plank of sufficient thickness and length, cutting away all the surplus wood with ordinary hollows and rounds, and this will leave a moulding of the exact dimensions of a cross-section through the metal forming the pocket. Now a block should be made of the exact dimensions shown in the working drawing and marked "Core" (see Fig. 24, *a* and *b*), and the prepared moulding should be glued to this block as shown in Fig. 24. A square joint at the corner is proper for this work. When dry, the corners should be smoothed up, making all parts of the mould meet and match. Next four holes should be bored at *c c c c*, Fig. 24 *b*, making the tenons just large enough to fit snugly into the holes. Then the entire work should be smoothed and polished making the parts which are to be iron jet black, and leaving the core prints in the natural wood. Following this a core box is to be made, which should be exactly of the dimensions and shape inside as shown by the working drawing. Such a box is shown in Fig. 25 and may be open top and bottom. In order to make a core in this box, the core maker puts the box together before him on the table. He then fills it with prepared sand and smoothes it off level with the top.

Core boxes are finished and polished on the inside only.

The next example is a casting which was made for a pump of some description. It is a cylinder which had a flange at one end and a pipe thread at the other (see Fig. 26). As in the previous example, the first thing required is the

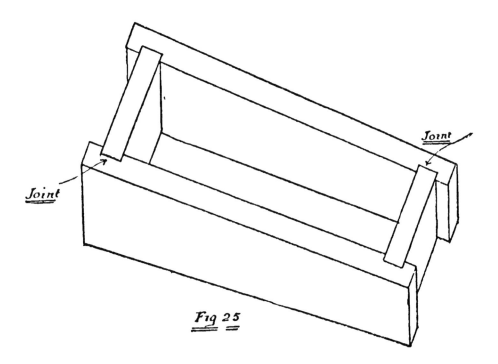

Fig 25

working drawing, which, as has already been stated, must show the casting, the core and the core prints. Fig. 27 shows a cross-section through the casting and core; this being the only drawing needed for making the pattern. This pattern was made by gluing together pieces of material of ordinary size, as a solid block suffi-

ciently large was not obtainable, and it was a
matter of no little difficulty to secure a piece of
material of sufficient diameter to turn up the

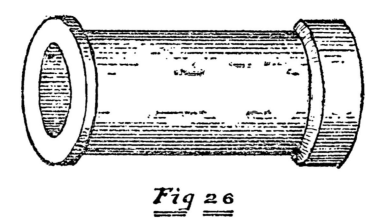

Fig 26

flange. It was also desirable that the pattern
should be divided in the middle without ripping
it through after turning it up. To accomplish

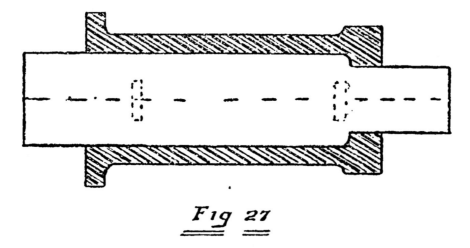

Fig 27

this the stock was prepared as shown in **Fig. 28,**
and in cross-section in Fig. 29. The pieces
a a were first doweled together and short
tenons, *d d*, made across the ends of the piece

and so fastened together in line with the joint. The gain for the flange piece, *b b*, was then cut to the desired depth clear around the piece,

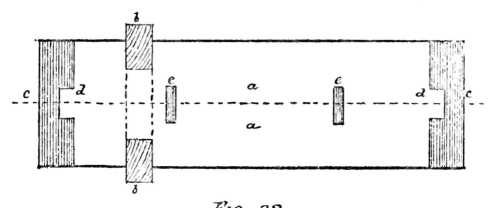

Fig 28
Longitudinal section through stock for Fig 26

and the flange pieces fitted in. The pieces, *a a*, were then taken apart and the flange pieces glued

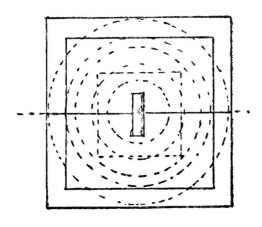

Fig 29
Cross section through stock for Fig 26

in their proper position, great care being exercised that no drops of fresh glue were left in the joint, otherwise the pattern would not have come apart when completed. Then the parts were put together again, grooves of proper size were then cut in the blocks *c c* to engage the short tenons *d d* and the blocks glued on to the ends of the work, as shown in Fig. 28. When thoroughly dry, the ends of the prepared stock were centered, the stock then put into the lathe and the pattern turned up, leaving the projecting ends, as shown in Fig. 27, for core prints, which come apart easily for the convenience of the moulder.

This pattern only requires half a core box, a longitudinal section of which is shown in Fig. 27; the cross-section describing a semicircle. Two pieces are used to make the core. Many moulders use ordinary flour paste to glue or cement their cores together. All such patterns should be painted in the parting just as shown in the working drawing, in order that the moulder may see at a glance just which part is to be metal and which core.[1]

Fig. 30 shows a cast pipe fitting which was

---

[1] All patterns should be painted so as to distinguish metal from core. Patterns for iron should be dark with light cores, and just the reverse for brass. All patterns are finished in shellac, rubbed to a polish.

used for steam heating. This fitting has been selected on account of its peculiar shape, which admits of making the entire pattern and part of the core box on the lathe.

Fig. 31 shows the working drawing, the first thing to be made in all cases before proceeding to make the pattern. By reference to this working drawing it will be seen that the straight parts *a* and *b* can be made by exactly the same process as described for making

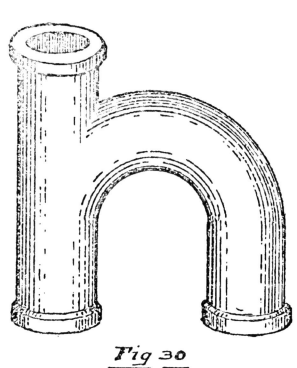

Fig 30

Fig. 27, with the exception that no flange is required. The circular portion *c* is turned out of a disc of proper size secured to the face plate and turned to a true semicircle in cross-section, as shown in Fig. 31½, which, being cut across through the line of its diameter and placed face to face, forms the half circular portion of the pattern c, Fig. 31. The only difficulty to be met with in making this pattern is the miter joint d, which is found by the intersection of parallel lines of equal distance from each other on the straight side, with similar circular lines struck from the center

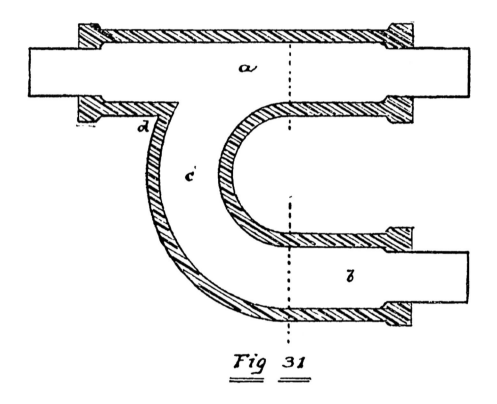

Fig 31

of the circular portion of the work. This is the common rule for mitering straight and curved mouldings.   Or the joint can be coped together, the circular part of the core box can be turned into the face of a plank of suitable size, which, when cut across the line of its diameter, forms the circular part of the core box.   The remainder will have to be carved out with gouges and the finished core box made as shown in Fig. 33. It will be observed that in this pattern a full core box is required, that is to say, two half core boxes, made right and left, and doweled together.

The next pattern treated is that of a double‑flanged wheel, for use on an overhead traveling crane. Reference to Fig. 34, *a* and

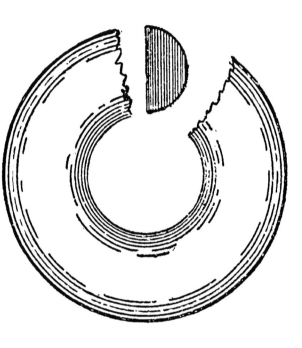

Fig 31½

b, which shows an elevation and cross-section, will afford a clear idea of this wheel.

There are so many ways to cast this wheel that it makes a nice illustration. The first thing to be considered is how to get it out of the sand, which problem we think is best solved in the manner shown in the working drawing, Fig. 35, A and B. By this method almost the entire wheel is cored out; but it is by no means an intricate task and is clearly illustrated in Fig. 36, which contains a sectional view of the finished pattern.

To make this pattern, cut out the discs *a a*, Fig. 36, of proper size for turning up.   To these

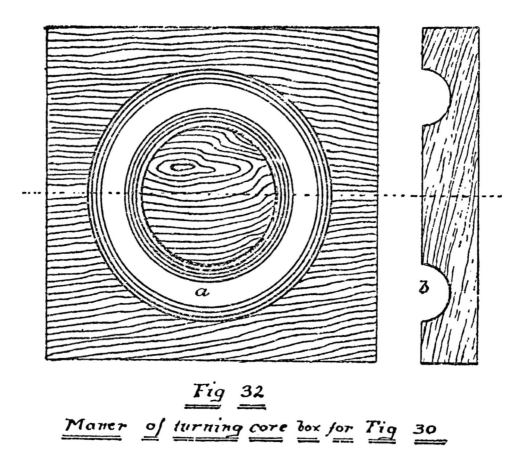

Fig 32

Manner of turning core box for Fig 30

discs glue the band *b* in sections, and to one disc the core print *c*.   Next attach the prepared discs to the lathe and turn up, as shown in cross-section, Fig. 36.   Turn up two core prints, *d d*, and dowel the two halves together, making the finished pattern.

Three core boxes are required for this pattern:
a plain half core for the center hole through the
wheel, which has already been explained; a core
box representing all the cavity between the spokes
of the wheel, Fig. 38, represented by the six

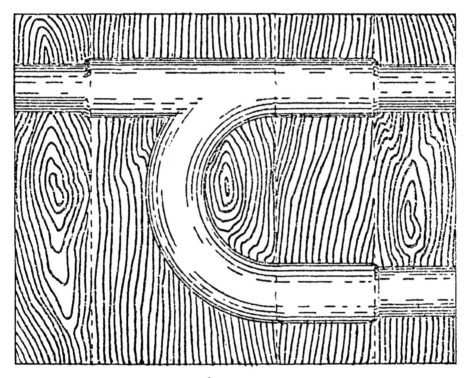

Fig 33
One half of core box for Fig 30

cores marked *b b*, Fig. 35, B, and a circular
core box turned into the face of a plank (see
Fig. 39, *a* and *b*), which will mould half of the
core *d* shown in Fig. 35, B.

A pattern for this wheel can be made without
coring out the flanges, by contriving the pattern

to part near one side or at any place which will permit the successful withdrawal of the half pattern. For a wheel cast after this pattern a three-part flask or a flask made of three boxes with a parting made between each box is employed. (See *a a*, Fig. 37.) It is possible to cast this

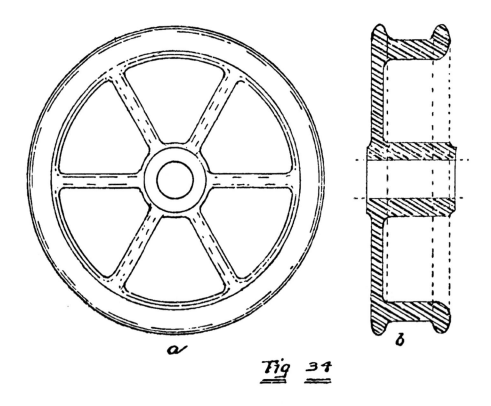

Fig 37

pattern in a two-part flask without any core whatever, and although this method is not recommended because of its greater cost and inferiority to other ways of doing the work, it is well that the pattern maker should be familiar with the process. To make this pattern the wheel should be made as shown in Fig. o34, with spokes and hub complete. The center hole, the hub, both sides of the rim and the spokes should have ample draft and the lower flange should be left loose so that the pattern will part at the line *a b*, Fig. o34.

To mould this pattern, the cope is laid down

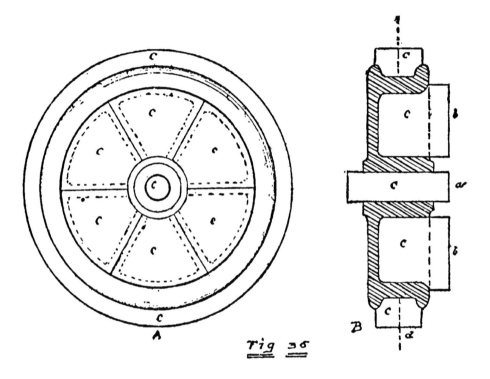

Fig 35

in an inverted position and filled about half full, or within about two inches of the top, and the sand smoothed down solid. The pattern is then turned with the spoke side up and pushed down hard into the sand. It is then taken out to see that the impression is perfect, and a parting is made at *i.* The pattern is then put back in its place and the parting *c-d* and *e-f* is made. The

sand is then filled in to *g-h* and a second parting
is made at *c-g n-f*.   Now the drag is put in place

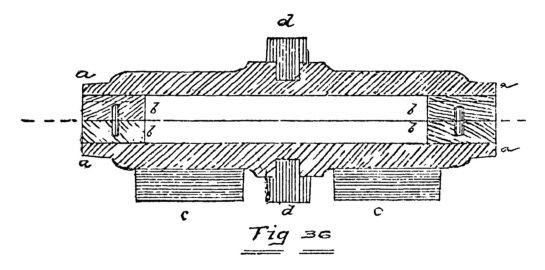

Fig 36

and rammed up.   The flask is then inverted and
the vents made, when the pattern will appear as
in Fig. o34.   The cope, which should part along

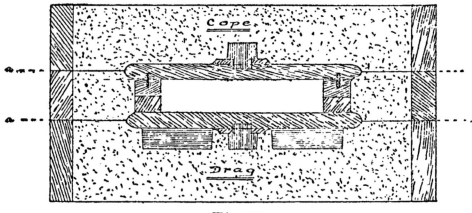

Fig 37
Showing how Fig 34 may be moulded in a two part flask

the line *c d i e f*, is now removed, as is also the
pattern from the line *a b* upwards.   The flask
should then be put together and turned over,

removing the drag, which should part along the line *c g h f*, after which the flange is removed. The flask is now put together again and turned over, which completes the work, and it is ready to receive the moulten metal. If the pattern is exactly right and the moulder is both expert and amiable, the casting can be made in this way,

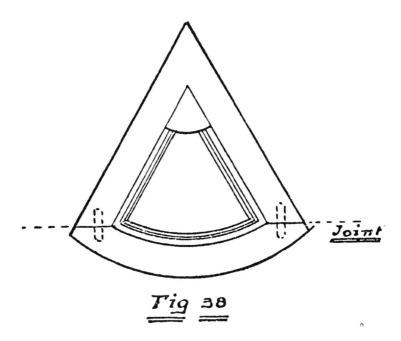

Fig 38

but this method is given more as an illustration of what can be done than as a sample of good pattern shop practice.

Many difficult or otherwise impossible forms can be cast by using a three-part flask. The double-flanged gear wheel, Fig. 40, *a* and *b*, is an illustration of work usually cast in a three-part flask. It can also be moulded in a two-part flask by making a double parting in the sand, as shown in Fig. 37. Or the gear can be cored into the wheel.

The next problem treated is that of an ordinary brake wheel or hand wheel, such as is used on freight cars, and which will serve more to illustrate wheel making in general than any

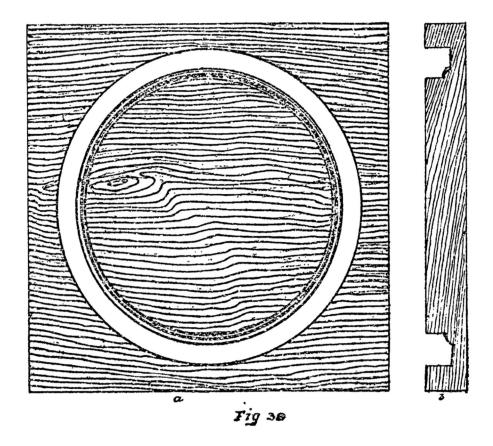

Fig 38

peculiarity in the construction of this particular piece. In this pattern, Fig. 41, nothing is required but a plain wooden wheel. The square hole in the center, being tapered, makes its own core.

When a great number of wheels are wanted the pattern is bedded half its depth in plaster of

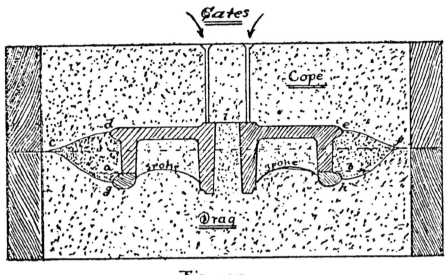

Fig 034

Cross section through mould showing wood pattern in the sand

Paris and the plaster cast so obtained is used for a follow board. This arrangement brings the

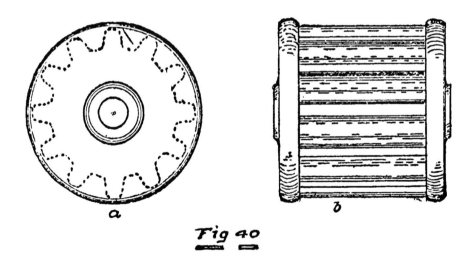

Fig 40

parting to the center of the pattern without the use of the trowel.

To make this pattern it is best to lay out on a plain board the design or outline, as shown in Fig. 41, dividing the rim into any number of equal parts. In this case there are six equal parts. One of these parts is a suitable pattern from which to saw out the rim, allowing a little extra wood on both sides for turning up. Having roughly sawed out the parts of the rim, fit the joints together, on the drawing or outline, taking care

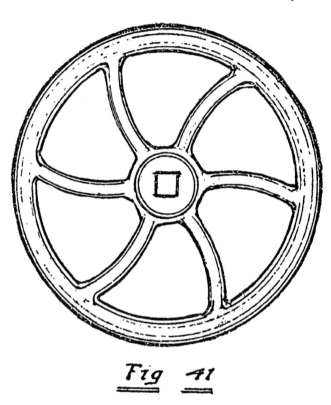

Fig 41

that the parts of the rim are so fitted together that they will describe in the rough as nearly as possible a perfect circle. Then glue the second layer on to the first, breaking joints with the sections, so as to form a rough ring, as shown in Fig. 42. Next secure this prepared ring to the face plate in proper position so that the tool will cut as nearly even all around as possible and turn up the ring so that it will be in cross-section, as shown in Fig. 43, using a thin wood or metal pattern to secure the desired shape. (See Fig. 43.) Now, with the turning chisel, mark the face plate lightly as a guide, in

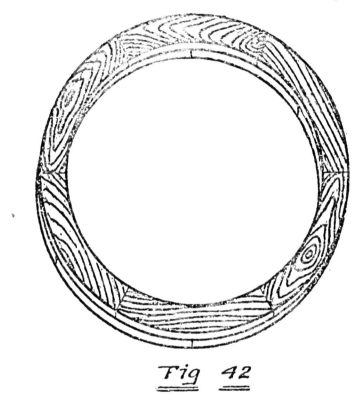

Fig 42

order that the ring may be turned over and yet be secured to the face plate in its exact former position. Another way to maintain the ring in its proper position when turning it over is to tack four little blocks or brackets to the face plate so that they will just touch the work to be turned over on either the inside or outside of the circle.

These blocks or brackets always bring the work
to its exact position in reversing. Now proceed
in like manner with the reverse side of the piece
and the result will be a round ring, which will
be round also
in cross-section.
Then get out
the hub of
proper dimen-
sions, mortise a
tapered square
hole in the cen-
ter for the brake
staff, cut six
gains in the hub
and in the rim
to receive the
ends of the
spokes, and se-
cure both hub
and rim in their

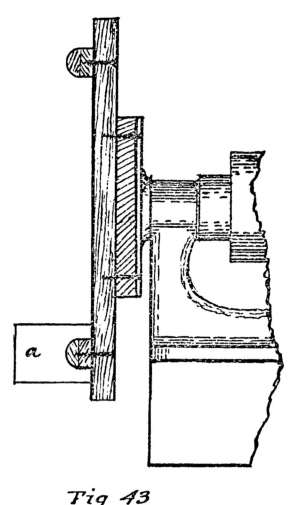

Fig 43

proper relative positions to the plank, using
the working drawing as a guide to put the
parts together. Provide six spokes of the desired form and fit them neatly into the gains.
All the parts should be snug and tight enough in

their adjustment to one another to require only a light blow to drive them home. (See Fig. 44.) Lastly finish up the spokes as desired and coat with black shellac varnish.

The making of cog or gear wheels is one of the most important features of the pattern

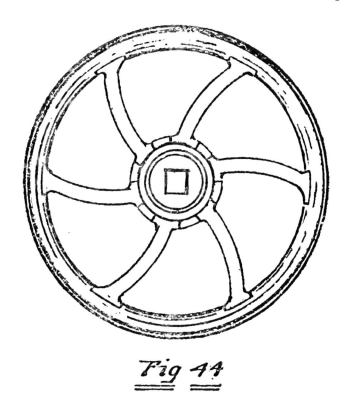

Fig 44

maker's trade, and although a drawing or blue print is usually provided in repair shops, the old cog wheel itself is sometimes given as a guide. A brief review of the principles of gear work and the technical terms employed by mechanics in relation to it will serve the purpose of this volume, inasmuch as every pattern maker should

possess a reasonable knowledge of the principles
and practical operation of the machinery in common use for which he may be at any time called
upon to produce patterns.

Gears are either straight or beveled.   Straight
gears are square on the face and transmit power
from one shaft to another one running parallel
to it.   Beveled gears have
their faces at an angle with
the line of the axis on which
they revolve, and transmit
power from one shaft to another running at an angle,
usually at a right angle, to
itself.   The pitch line of a
gear wheel is an imaginary
line running around the wheel
through the cogs at a point

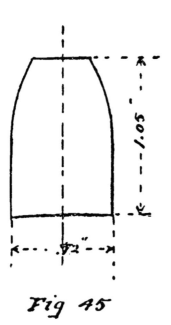

Fig 45

which is governed by the number and size
of the teeth.   The pitch diameter would be
the diameter of the wheel at this imaginary
line.   This pitch line is located at the point
where the wheels would touch each other if,
instead of being toothed or cogged, they were
plain friction wheels.   The circular pitch of
a gear wheel is the distance from center to

center of the cogs on the pitch line, and is found
by dividing the pitch line into as many spaces as
there are cogs in the wheel. All calculations in
reference to gear wheels are made from the pitch
line. Cogs are always .7 of the circular pitch in
length, of which .4 lies inside and .3 outside of
the pitch line. The thickness of any cog is
always $\frac{48}{100}$ of the circular pitch. (See Fig. 46.)

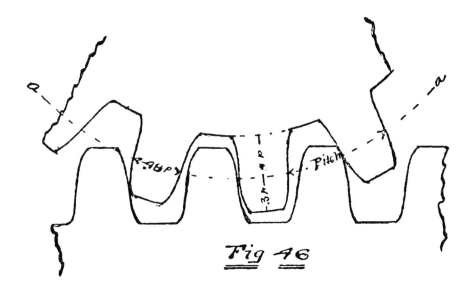

Fig 46

Let it be assumed of a gear wheel of any convenient size, that it is 21 inches in diameter at
the pitch line, with any convenient number of
teeth, say 44. For all practical purposes an
accurate measurement of the circumference of
this wheel would be accepted as 66 inches[1] at the
pitch line, and the pitch $66 \div 44 = 1.5$ inches.

---

[1] The decimal is 65.9736.

The root of the tooth—that part inside of the pitch line—being .4 of the circular pitch, would give 1.5″×.4=.6 of an inch inside of the pitch line as the base of the tooth.   Now, as it is customary to make a gear wheel plain and then glue the cogs to the face of the rim, it follows that the radius of the wheel would be the radius of the pitch line, minus the root of the tooth, or .6 of an inch, making the wheel at the base of the tooth 1.2 of an inch (.6+.6=1.2) less in diameter than 21 inches, or 19.8 inches.   Then the total length of a cog, being .7 of the circular pitch, equals 1.5×.7=1.05 inches, which is the length of this particular tooth.   Its thickness being .48 of the circular pitch gives 1.5×.48=.72 inches as the thickness of the tooth on the pitch line. Hence the solution of the problem calls for a wheel 19.8 inches in diameter, to the outside surface of which, at regular intervals, determined by accurate measurement, there should be glued cogs or teeth which are 1.05 inches in length and .72 inches thick at the pitch line.

All wheels are more or less alike; therefore it would be superfluous to treat the minor problems of wheel patterns in this work, as every workman who understands the general principles involved will use his own judgment and discretion in such cases, especially as the nature of the work, the size of the wheel, the strength of parts, etc., will always be the controlling factor in the construction.

Assuming that there has been constructed a wheel which has been turned to exactly 19.8 inches diameter by the shrinkage rule and the face of which has sufficient draft, the surface is divided into 44 equal parts by scribing square across the face of the work, with a pointed instrument or penknife, and marking the scribes on the sides of the rim. The teeth are gotten out to approximately the proper shape and size. Then into a piece of thin hardwood a hole is made exactly the shape of the desired tooth. The teeth should then be carefully finished with hand tools so that they will just pass through this hole, allowing a very little draft in each tooth and marking the tooth in such manner as to easily distinguish the allowance made when the work is being glued together, in order that the draft may all be the right way. An exact center mark should be made on each end of the cog, matching exactly the marks on the rim of the wheel. Next the cogs should be glued to place, using care that the center of each cog is exactly with the dividing marks on the wheel. Small brads are used to hold the parts in place until the glue dries, and when thoroughly dry the work should be dressed up with sandpaper and a small fillet of beeswax run along both sides of the base of the tooth, pressing it in place with an irod rod which has been warmed over a spirit lamp. To finish, shellac varnish, as before described, is used.

Patterns of this class are usually parted by the moulder's trowel along the center of the spoke and at one edge of the rim.

Fig. 47 represents a pair of miter gear wheels in mesh. Beveled gear work may be either a mitered gear wheel as shown (in which case the pitch line is at an angle of 45° from the shaft, such a gear transmitting power from one shaft to another at equal speed); or, in cases where a different speed is required, one wheel will be larger than the other (in which case it, the pitch line, will be any angle which the nature of the case may require). The making of a miter or beveled gear pattern, while not necessarily a very difficult piece of work, requires persistent care and skill. The pitch of a beveled gear is an imaginary line, *a a*, Fig. 47, which line represents the surface of cones working as plain friction wheels. Any variation in the relative sizes of these two cones would also change the angle

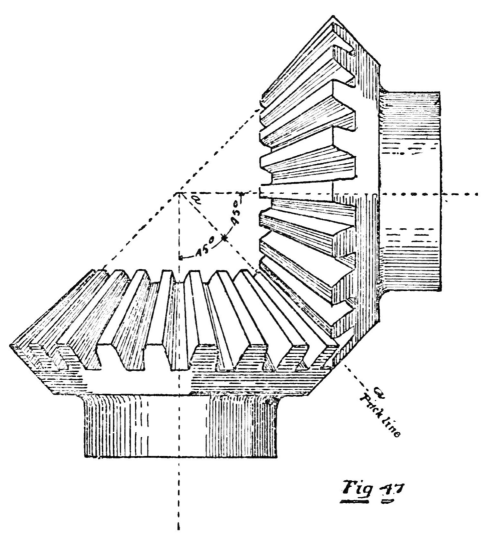

Fig 47

of the pitch from the axis of the wheels. To change the angle of the axis from a right angle would also determine the angle of the pitch line. To more fully illustrate the manner of laying out Fig. 47, see Fig. 47½. Here *a b* and *a c* represent the axis on which the gear revolves and *a a* the pitch line. Assuming, for convenience of calculation, that the pitch diameter *d-e* and *d-f* are 7 inches in length and the number of teeth 22, the circumference at the pitch diameter

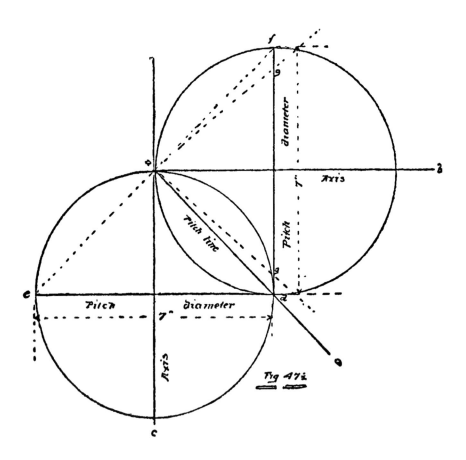

will be 22 inches* and the circular pitch at this point 1 inch. Hence by measuring in .4 of an inch at a right angle from the pitch line *a-a*, and *a-f* at the pitch diameter, the profile of a cone is obtained to which the teeth or cogs may be

---

* The exact decimal is 21.9912.

glued with accuracy and precision. The calculation for both ends of the teeth should be made
by the rules given for gear work, i.e., turn up the
cone and lay it off into 22 equal spaces, square
up for the centers of the teeth with the centering
tool (Fig. 48), glue the centers of the cogs to the

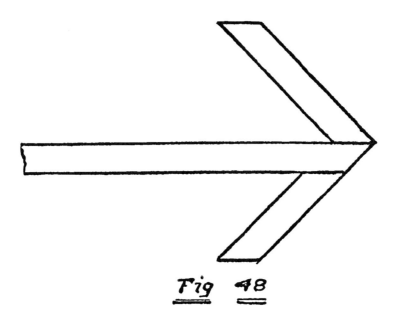

Fig 48

centers so established and finish in the usual
manner.

Fig. 49, showing an iron dome with projecting
ornament at the top and a handle at each side, is
here introduced as a sample of what may be
done with hollow cores. Assume that a rough
form has been glued up as shown in cross-section
in Fig. 50. Attach this form to the lathe and
turn out the inside first, otherwise it will be im-

possible to turn that part. Reverse the pattern and finish the outside, as shown by the shaded portion in Fig. 50, and attach square core prints

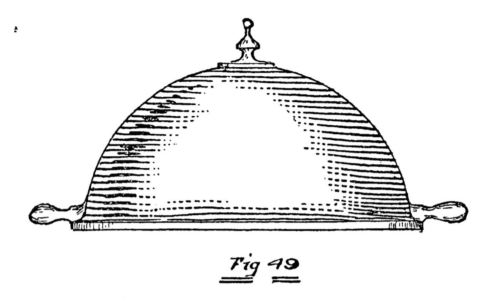

Fig 49

for the handles and finial. Make suitable core boxes for these prints, which core boxes should

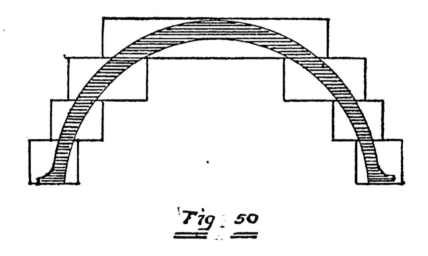

Fig. 50

be constructed so that the bottom of the box is the center of the core. In this case the cores go together just the reverse of the ordinary way.

Next turn out the handles and finial of the desired form, rip them apart and fasten the halves into the bottom of the core boxes as in Fig. 52. A core moulded in one of these boxes will have an impression of half of this turned piece in the face, and when the two halves are pasted together

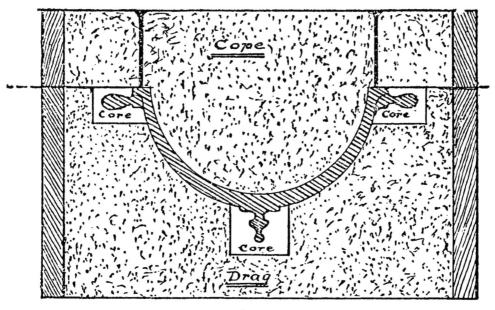

Fig 51
Cross section through flask showing metal & cores

a proper cavity is left to mould the desired form, which can then be put into the cavities in the sand left by the core prints on the pattern, and which will then appear as in Fig. 51. In this pattern it will be necessary to make special provisions for supporting the sand in the cope, otherwise it will have a tendency to fall off in han-

dling.   Iron kettles with flaring legs and round
ears are cast in this manner.   Others have the
leg straight on one side so it will draw readily,
and the ear is made in two pieces, which are
loose from the pattern and remain in the sand
until the pattern is withdrawn.   It is well to
remember that any projecting part of a casting
which is of such a shape that it can of itself be
drawn out of the sand, may often be left loose

Fig 52

Cross section through core boxes for Fig 51

when on account of some angle it is prevented
from being drawn with the pattern, in which
case it remains in the sand until the pattern is
drawn, after which it is easily taken out.

There are many patterns which from some
peculiar formation are much easier to mould if a
special follow board is made for them, and on
account of a delicate form of construction are
much easier to make by first making a follow
board of the desired shape and then building

the pattern up piece by piece upon this form; for instance, the curved grates in stoves, the cast basket racks in passenger cars, etc., etc. Especially is this true of small, curved open work castings, where it would be tedious, not to say impossible, for the moulder to make a nice parting in the sand with the trowel. By the use of a follow board, which exactly fits the plain side

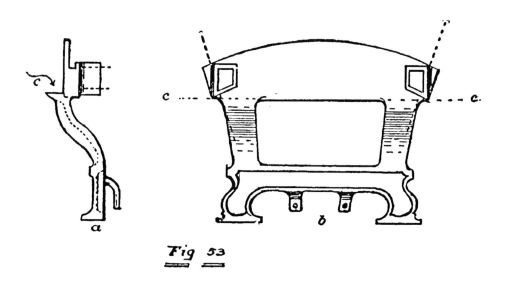

Fig 53

of the casting, the parting is made without any trouble. As an example of a pattern of this kind the aisle end for a car seat has been selected. This pattern was arranged in such a manner as to be divided in the middle, so that the upper portion is cast separate from the leg and used for the wall end of the seat. (See Fig. 53, *a* and *b*.)

The first step in this case was to make up the follow board (Fig. 54), on which the aisle

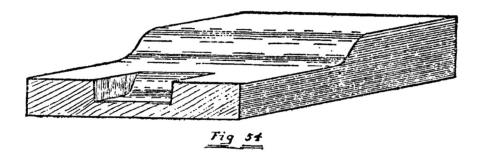

Fig 54

end was laid out full size, taking dimensions on a straight-edge and carrying them over

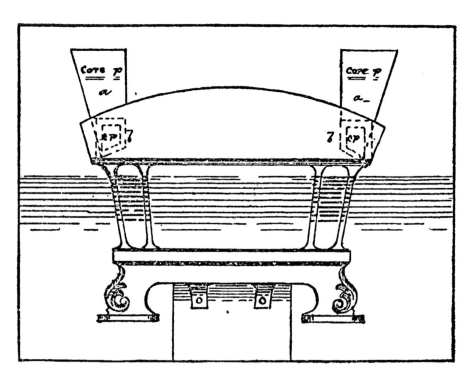

Fig 55
Shows finished pattern in place on follow board

to the curved surface. In cases where the finished pattern had to project below the face of this follow board, as shown by the core prints *a-a* and the sockets for the seat rails *b b* in Fig. 55, the wood was mortised out to the desired depth. After this the pattern was gotten out piece by piece, fitted to the board in its proper place and secured with small sprigs until the glue joints hardened, care being taken not to glue the pattern proper to the follow board. In this case it was necessary to allow the arm, which carried the back cushion from side to side in reversing the seat, to pass behind the socket *b b*, Fig. 55, thus making it necessary to core out a slot between the socket for the seat rail and the aisle end, which was done as shown by the cores *a a*, Fig. 55. These are samples of balanced cores, which will be explained further on.

This pattern has a joint at *ccc*, Fig. 53, so that it may be cast without the leg being made fast against the wall of the car.

CASTING WITH PART PATTERNS, SWEEPS, OPEN SAND WORK, ETC.

Castings are sometimes made without regular patterns, or with only a portion of the pattern. Some castings are made by the use of straight-edges, curves, etc. Other castings are made with sweeps. Many of these methods have come down to us from periods of remote antiquity.

Recently in the foundry of ——— at ——— the moulders were making a slab of iron 2 feet wide and 5 feet long, with a rim around the under edge and V-shaped cross bars or ribs on the under side at intervals of about 6 inches each way. (See Fig. 56, *a b*.)

There was no pattern for this work at all; but instead there were some 1×2 inch strips and a straight plank, with a V-shaped edge. To make this mould, the floor of the foundry was leveled off with the straight-edge, the grooves rubbed into the sand with the V-shaped edge of the board and the 1×2 inch strip laid down to form the line of the outside of the casting. Against these the sand was packed level with their tops and smoothed off. The cope was made with a straight edge.

A very simple and useful "kink" was employed recently in the case of a large piece of machinery which was damaged in shipping. It had a large circular gear about 8 feet across without spokes or hub which was broken in two or three pieces. This was an old, out-of-date machine and it was

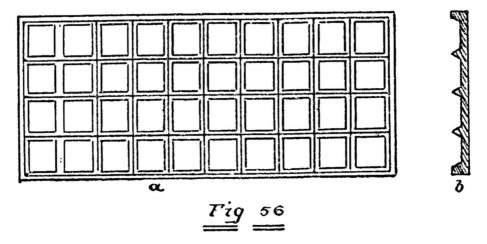

a   *b*

Fig 56

not possible to procure a gear from the original pattern and it was considered too expensive to make a new one, as only one casting was required. In this emergency the services of an expert pattern maker were enlisted. This workman prepared a pattern of one-sixth of the gear, which he fixed to two wooden bars, so arranged as to swing around a center pin in the top of a stake, which was driven firmly into the floor of the foundry. (See Fig. 57.)

To make the mould from this partial pattern, level off the foundry floor with a straight-edge. The center stake is then driven and left standing up above the floor the thickness of the casting. The partial pattern is next put on the center pin and rammed up, leaving both ends open. After

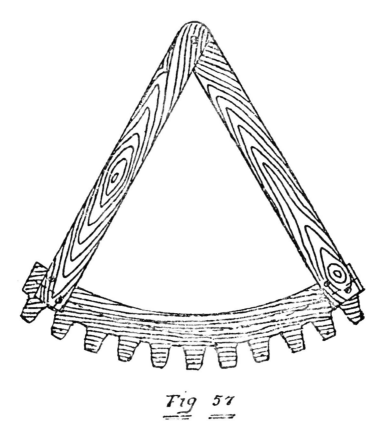

Fig 57

this it is lifted and moved, taking care that the last cog on the pattern exactly fits the impression in the sand. Ram this up again and move the pattern as before. Continue this until the complete circle is made, which will be an impression of the complete gear. Since seeing this I have used the same plan for making mud rings for boilers with perfect success, thereby saving much valuable time and material. This method is not recommended in general practice; but where a single casting is all that will ever be needed, the

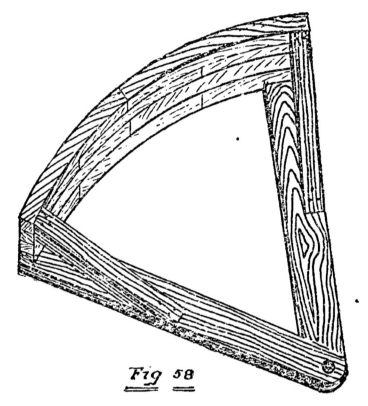

Fig 58

making of an entire pattern can and in some cases should be avoided.

Another problem of a similar nature is found in making a large pulley or flywheel where the cost of making the pattern is not justified by the number of wheels required. To make the mould for such a pulley, first construct the form of the radius desired for the rim of the wheel (see Fig.

58), and in case of a belt wheel, make the rim of the shape desired to hold the belt centrally on the face of the pulley. Now secure this form to two arms so fixed as to cause it to swing around

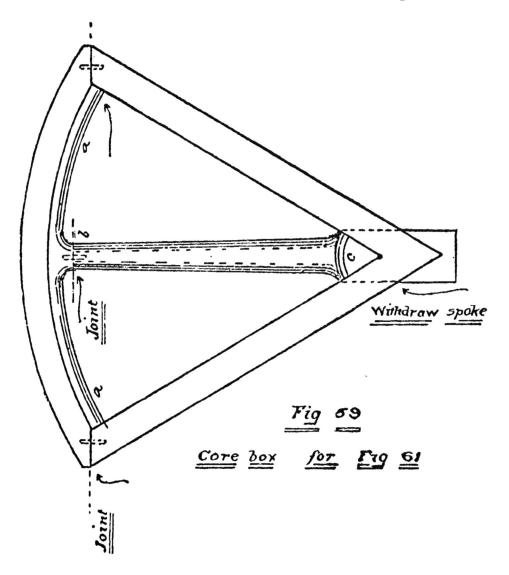

Fig 59

Core box for Fig 61

a center stake at the proper radius. Make up a core box of exactly the shape of one-sixth of the wheel inside of the rim; that is, the radius of the outside of the core box should be the thickness of the rim less than the radius of the form. Get out the rib, *a-a*, Fig. 59, and glue it in place. Turn up a hub one-half its length, cut it in six parts and glue two of the pieces into the apex of the core box, as in *c*, Fig. 59, leaving a slot or mortise for withdrawing the spoke. Make one spoke and secure the joint with a dowel pin at *b*, Fig. 59. This will be better understood by a

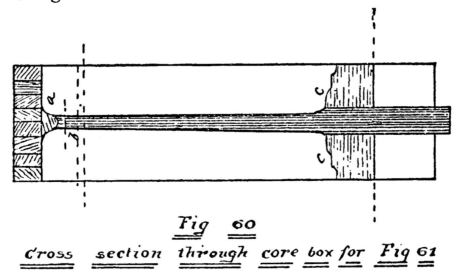

Fig 60

Cross section through core box for Fig 61

study of Fig. 60. A round core is also required for the center hole. The center stake should be turned up of proper size so that when drawn out or driven down it will leave a print for the center core.

To make a mould from this set of patterns, first make six cores in the core box (see Fig. 59 and Fig. 60), and one round core for the center. Level off the floor of the foundry and drive the

center stake down level. Then put in a small
iron center pin and set the form (Fig. 58) on it.
Bank the sand solidly against the outside of the

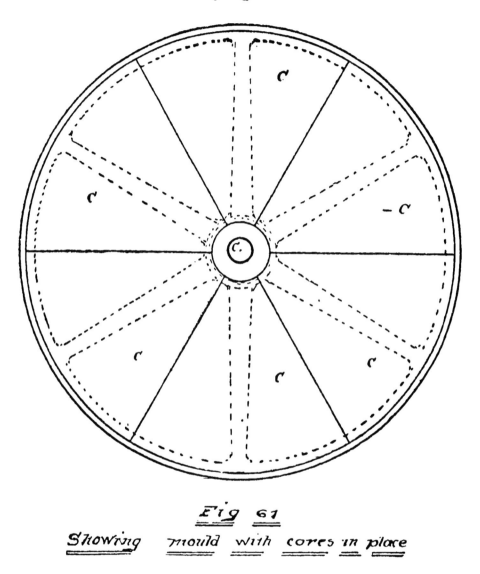

Fig 61

Showing   mould with cores in place

pattern, level with the top, moving the form and
continuing the operation until a complete circular
pit is formed of the depth of the pattern. Remove the form and the center stake, leaving as
much of the hole made by removing the stake as

is required for a core print for the center hole. Place the six prepared cores in position, taking care that the proper thickness of the rim is maintained clear around the wheel. Place the center core in position, pushing it down until it is level with the face of the wheel. The finished mould is shown in Fig. 61.

SWEEP WORK

Sweep work or swept up moulds are moulds made entirely without a pattern, and can only be used for circular forms which, for reasons of economy or otherwise, it may be deemed expedient to have cast without the expense of a pattern. The sweeps are nothing more than plain plank cut to the desired form and arranged to revolve around a stake driven into the floor of the foundry. The sand is packed in front of the sweep and the sweep moved around, thus scraping the surplus sand away until the desired form is obtained. Sweeps are beveled on the edge so as to push or pack the sand ahead of them as they move around the center stake. There are various ways of making and using sweeps. The ordinary way to sweep a pattern, where the form is such as to admit of doing so, as shown in Fig. 63, is to make a sweep of the exact form of the outside of the casting and another one that is exactly the thickness of the casting, but deeper. On the second sweep the form and thickness of the metal is painted black. (See Fig. 64, *a*.)

It will be seen that this pair of sweeps are so arranged as to form a rabbet in the sand, which insures the cope being centrally located.

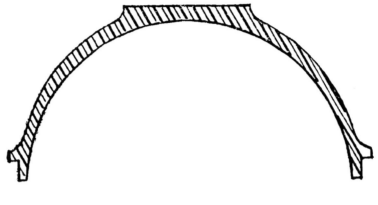

Fig 62

To make a mould for Fig. 63 with this set of sweeps, the floor of the foundry is first leveled off and a stake driven down, leaving enough

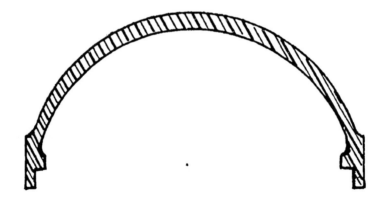

Fig 63

above ground to operate the sweep. The first sweep is then put on, the sand packed about the stake and a hill is formed representing the outside of the casting. When complete, a parting is made and the cope placed in position and rammed up. Gates are then made and the cope removed. The second sweep is now substituted for the first and the sweeping continued until a perfect form is produced of the inside of the casting. Now the sweep is removed, the cope placed in position and the mould is complete.

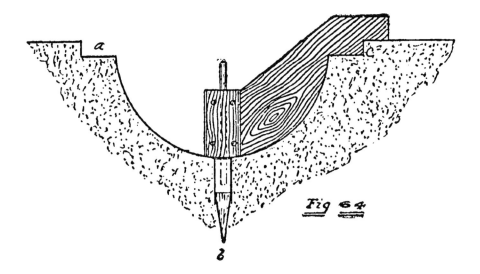

Fig 64.

A much more difficult operation is one where the casting is of such a form that it is impossible to lift the cope from the outside. (See Fig. 62.) In this instance a hole is swept into the drag—or foundry floor, as the case may be—having the form of the inside of the casting. (See Fig. 64.) The cope is then placed in position, rammed up and removed. The second sweep is then placed on the stake and the sweeping continued until a perfect form of the outside of the casting is obtained. (See Fig. 65.) The stake and sweeps being removed and the cope placed in position, the mould is complete. The difficulty in this case is in handling the cope, for which special

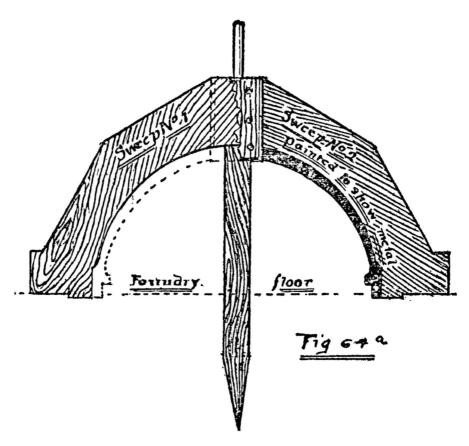

Fig 64 a

A pair of ordinary sweeps

arrangements should be made for supporting the sand.

It is possible, for certain special work, to sweep both cope and drag; but it is seldom done.

There are various reasons for using sweep

work, the first and most common of which is from a consideration of economy, as where a pattern is large and costly and only one or more

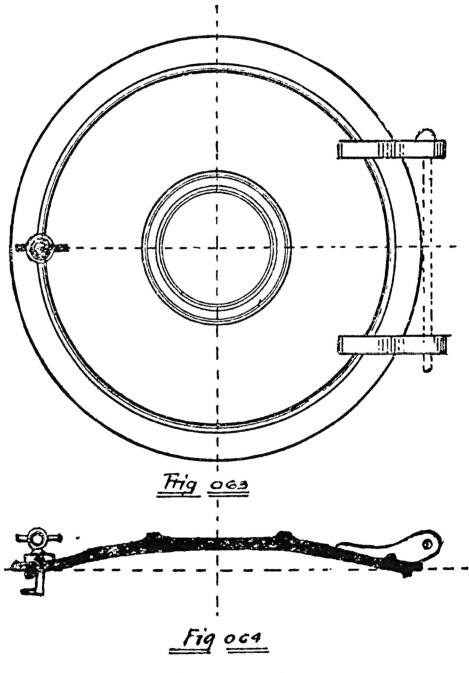

Fig 063

Fig 064

Cross section through smoke box door

pieces are required, it is often better to use
sweeps, as they save the cost of making a pattern. The cost of moulding from sweeps, how-

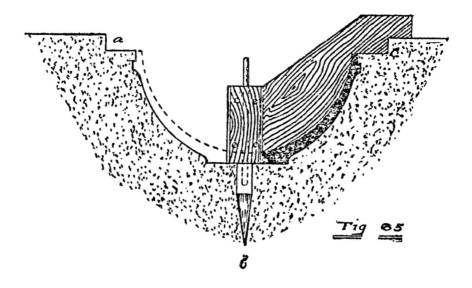

Fig 65

ever, is more than from a pattern, and in very
heavy work the saving of the extra cost would
pay for the pattern. It is possible to sweep a

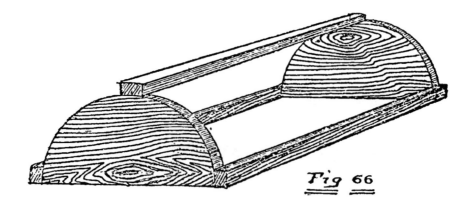

Fig 66

pattern which will not draw in the ordinary
manner, also circular castings having projections
of various kinds may be swept by having wood

patterns of the projecting parts. To illustrate
this is cited an instance of a casting which was
made at the Frisco R. R. shops last winter at Cape
Girardeau, Mo. This casting was the door on

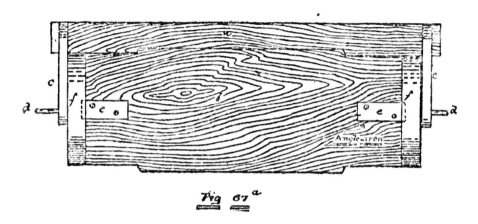

Fig 67 ᵃ

the front of an engine, usually termed "the smoke
box door." It was required to cast hinges on
this door, together with some other minor projections not necessary to illustrate. The first thing
done was to make, on a
piece of heavy manila paper,
a regular working drawing
in cross-section of the required casting. (See Fig.
064.) Then the perpendicular line *a b* for
the center of the sweep was drawn. The
sweeps can be laid out by pricking through
the drawing. The upper line gives the shape
of sweep No. 1 and the lower one sweep

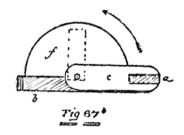

Fig 67 ᵇ

No. 2. A face view of this casting is given
for the purpose of locating the hinges, etc.
(See Fig. 063.)   Next wood patterns of the

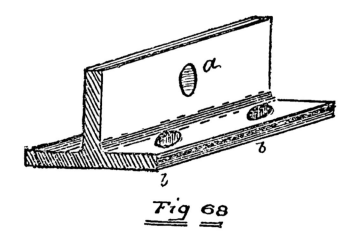

Fig 68

hinges were made, leaving the pivot holes to
be drilled after the casting was completed.
Then into a suitable drag box or the foundry
floor a stake was driven to such a point

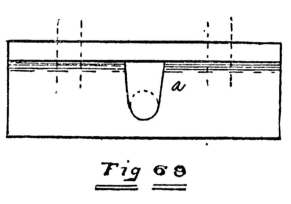

Fig 69

as to allow No. 1
to turn freely
with the outer
end at the part-
ing in the box
or floor. Then
the sand was
packed and the sweeps moved until the form
was perfectly true and complete. Next a
parting with dry sand was made in the usual
way and the wood patterns were set in position,

care being taken that they were exactly in position, where they could be secured by packing a little sand around them. Now the cope was put on and rammed up, great care being taken not to move the hinges. Next the cope and hinge patterns, which remained in the cope, were removed. Now the center stake was

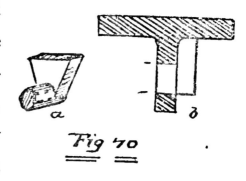

Fig 70

driven down exactly the thickness of the casting by measurement, and sweep No. 2 was put on, which cut away exactly the size and shape of the required casting. Then the

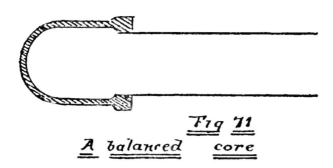

Fig 71

A balanced core

stake and the sweep were removed, the cope replaced and the mould was finished.

To lay out any sweep, it is only necessary to make a full-sized working drawing of the desired casting. Then look carefully at this drawing and see just how it ought to lie in the mould.

Then turn the drawing that side up. The upper line of the drawing is sweep No. 1 and the lower line is sweep No. 2, which also has the line of No. 1 laid out on it and the shape of the metal painted black. It is also customary to add an angle to both sweeps, as shown at c in Fig. 65. This acts as a guide for gauging the thickness of the metal and insures proper locating of the cope.

It is frequently a matter of great convenience to be able to sweep up quickly a large core, such as for the cylinder of a locomotive or other hollow work where nothing more than a plain, straight core is required. This can easily be done by the use of two half-circles of plank of the desired radius, secured in position with three strips of wood, as shown in Fig. 66. The core is packed in this frame and swept off with a straight-edge. Or it may be required to sweep up a straight, round core of different diameters, having offsets, etc. To do this, get out a plank which is of the shape and size of a longitudinal section through the center of the core, as at b in Fig. 67a, allowing for the thickness of the half circles f f. Fasten the half circles f f in place, and if possible secure them from warping with good heavy angle irons let in flush with the wood, as at *c c*, Fig. 67*a*. Now get out a sweep, *a*, Fig. 67*a*, which exactly fits the side of this plank or bottom board. Hang the sweep by the two arms *c c* to the center pins *d d*; all of which will be easily understood by referring to Fig. 67*a* and Fig. 67*b*. The sweep *a* should be beveled on both sides towards the center on the working edge, so that it will press the sand in as

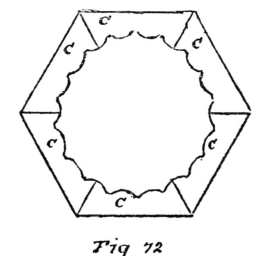

Fig 72
Mould for fluted column made entirely of cores

it passes back and forth over it. To make a half core on this device it is only necessary to pack the sand on the bottom board and pass the sweep *a* backwards and forwards over it, filling in sand until the desired form is obtained.

Fig. 68 is designed to illustrate the manner in which bolt holes, etc., are moulded at right angles to each other through a casting. By referring to the drawing, Fig. 68, it will be observed that the holes *b b*, if slightly tapered so they can be drawn out of the sand, will leave their own core; while the hole *a*, Fig. 68, will not draw out of the sand with any core yet described. For all such work a peculiar core and core box, called a stop core, are used. For this purpose a peculiarly shaped core print is put on the pattern, as shown in Fig. 69. It then becomes necessary to make a core box which will mould a core as shown at *a* in Fig. 70. At *b*, Fig. 70, is shown a cross-section through the casting, with the core in place.

In many cases it is necessary to use cores which, from some peculiarity of the design, will have no support at one end and have a tendency to fall down, or at least sag enough to make the casting thin on one side. In such cases the core and core print are made long enough for the core to lie in the core print without tipping down. These are called balance cores. (See Fig. 71.) In other cases cores may be so long as to sag of their own weight. When this is liable to occur, small iron pieces called "bridges" are put under them. These fuse with the heat of the metal and become part of the casting. In some instances it is necessary to nail the core in place to keep it from floating.

In cases of very complicated designs it is sometimes more convenient to make the actual mould for the casting entirely of cores, in which event the pattern would bear little resemblance to the casting, but would, instead, have the form of the cavity in the sand which would be required to hold in position the cores, forming the actual mould.   As an instance of this, observe Fig. 72, which shows a cross-section through such a mould, made for casting a fluted column.   In this instance the pattern would be a plain hexagon.   This is only referred to as being one of the many possibilities of pattern making and is not cited as being ordinary shop practice.

Having covered pretty thoroughly the common every-day problems which come to an ordinary pattern shop, a pattern is now illustrated which, when properly made, is a simple matter; yet before the reasonable solution of this problem was found, it had cost the firm doing the work a large sum of money.   The problem was to cast a triple locomotive chime whistle, having three separate compartments of different lengths in the bell, and three chambers for steam in the base.

This pattern was first made, or rather attempted, and some three or four whistles were cast from it. It was so complicated a piece of work that an ordinary moulder could not put it together and get a mould from it; in consequence it had always to be taken to the foundry by the pattern maker. The foundry made a labor charge of $5.00 on this work, in addition to the weight of the brass, for each and every whistle cast. Having decided that some improvement could be made in this pattern, it was sent to the shop and remodeled and some slight improvements were made. However, it yet remained a very unsatisfactory piece of work. It was given

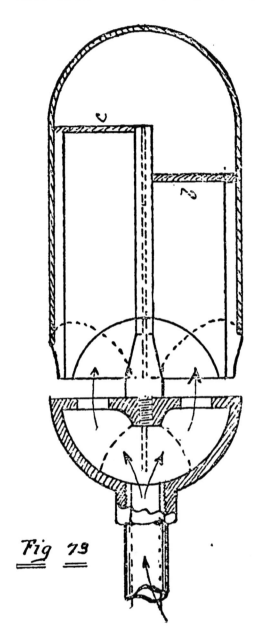

Fig 73

to C. W. Sherwood, now of Racine, Wis., who produced the pattern as here shown, which has proven very satisfactory in its operation.

A clear idea of this casting may be derived by reference to Figs. 73, 74 and 75. Fig. 73 shows a cross-section through the bell of the whistle and the base, both of which are hollow and in three compartments.

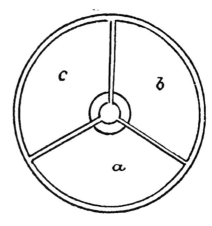

Fig 74

Cross section of bell

The first compartment extends the full length of the bell; the next is shorter, extending to c, Fig. 73, and the third still shorter, extending to b, Fig. 73. In proceeding with a work of this kind, the first requisite is a working drawing of full size, and one which should be as nearly complete in every detail as it is

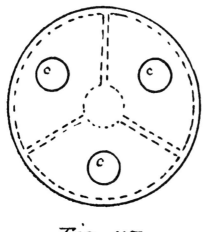

Fig 75

Cross section of base

possible to make. Next make the pattern for the bell, Fig. 76, and the base, Fig. 77. Now make the core box as shown at *a-b* in Fig. 78, two slides, *c-c*, Fig. 78, being made for

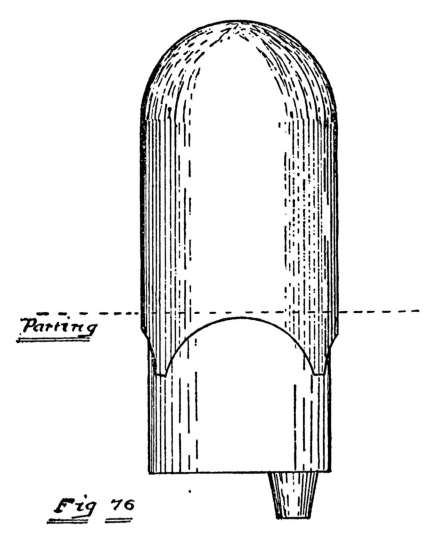

Parting

Fig 76

the openings at the upper end. One slide reaches almost across the opening and joins with the partition slide *d*, Fig. 79. The other cuts off even with the inside of the core box and is only designed for closing up the slot when not needed. Next make the partition slides *d*, Fig. 79, one for the middle partition *c* and one for the short partition *b*, Fig. 79. Now make two more slides *e e*, which are the duplicates of the slides *d d*, except that they cut off at the inside of the core box. These also are only used to stop up the slot when not in use. Next make a center pin *d*, Fig. 78, and rip it in halves, cutting out the little gain *e*, Fig. 79, so that the sweep *g g*, Fig. 79, can work clear down to the bottom of the bell of the whistle in sweeping out the half partition *c c*, Fig. 79. These centers should be made right

Fig 77

and left, in order that the core box may reverse. At *f*, Fig. 78, is a half plug which is changed over in reversing the core box. The holes *bb-bb*, Fig. 79, are made so that a small iron rod may be driven up into the core to prevent it from breaking apart. Fig. 80 is a cross-section of the core box for the base of the whistle. The box may be made in only two parts by allowing a little draft at *e*, Fig. 80.

The top b is turned up, as shown, and the partitions d d d glued to it. The cores c-c, Fig. 80,

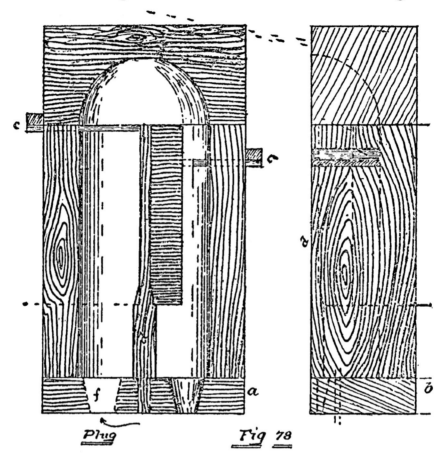

Plug   *Fig 78*

make the vent holes c c c, Fig. 75, which let the steam out into the bell of the whistle.

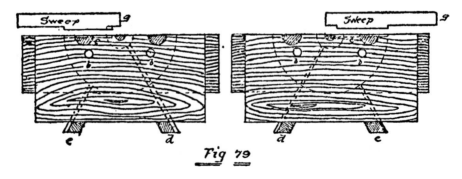

Fig 79

There is a variety of cast parts used in locomotive and car work, such as draw bars, truck pedestals, oil boxes, etc. These castings, while apparently very common and rough to look at, call

for considerable skill in the making of the pattern. As a sample, an ordinary oil box has been selected. (See Fig. 81.) This will be more fully understood

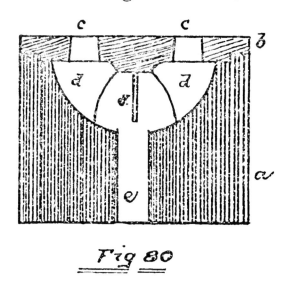

Fig 80

by studying the two sectional views of the castings, Figs. 82 and 83. A complete working

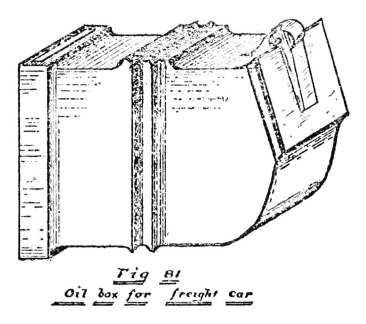

Fig 81
Oil box for freight car

drawing is shown in Figs. 84 and 85. To make this pattern, first prepare the working drawing on heavy paper and prick out the outlines complete and transfer them to a plank of proper size. With this plank as a pattern, cut enough mate-

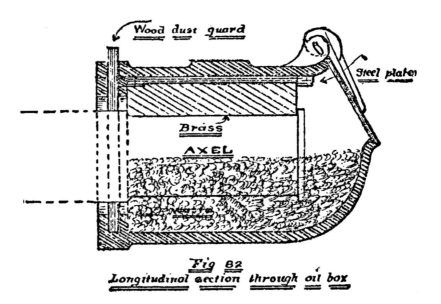

Fig 82
Longitudinal section through oil box

rial to build up a block of the entire thickness of the core, making the parting in the center.

Fig 83
Cross section through oil box

Next get out two side pieces of sufficient thickness to complete the pattern. (See a b, Fig.85.) Now dowel the two center pieces together and glue up the remainder and this will form a block roughly resembling the desired pattern. Then carve this into the required form with the paring tools, gouges, etc., and when finished

paint the inside as in Fig. 86. The core print
a, Fig. 86, and the hinge for the lid *b*, Fig. 86,

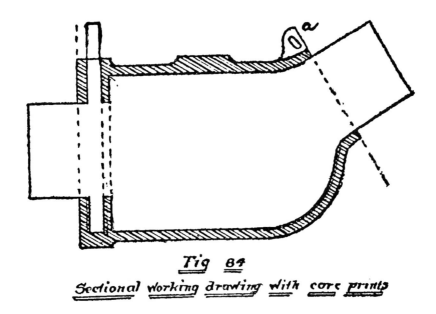

Fig 84
Sectional working drawing with core prints

should be added to the original block. This
hinge may also have the slot for the lid cored
through it in the ordinary way; that is, by put-

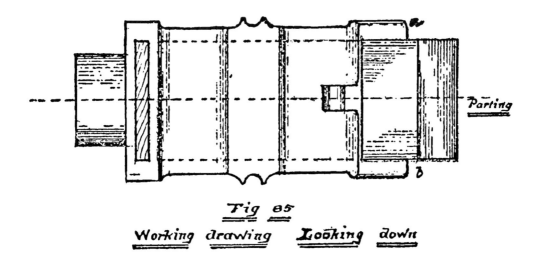

Fig 85
Working drawing Looking down

ting the necessary core print on the outside of
the hinge piece, but this cannot be illustrated

in this view of the pattern.   Next make a complete core box, as shown by the working drawing. Half of such a core box is shown in Fig. 87. Little strips of wood *a*, Fig. 87, or blocks *b*, Fig. 87, can be tacked into the core for any

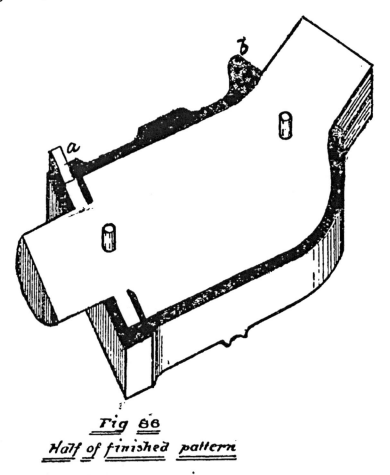

Fig 88
Half of finished pattern

slides, projections, etc., that may be required by the nature of the work.   A rather neat piece of work is a double-flanged elbow for a steam pipe, as shown in Fig. 88.   Assuming this to be for a small pipe, say 4-inch, it becomes a simple piece of lathe work.   Having made a proper

working drawing (Fig. 89) for determining the size
of the parts to be made, prepare a piece of material
of suitable dimensions from which to turn out a
ring, which should be a perfect semicircle in

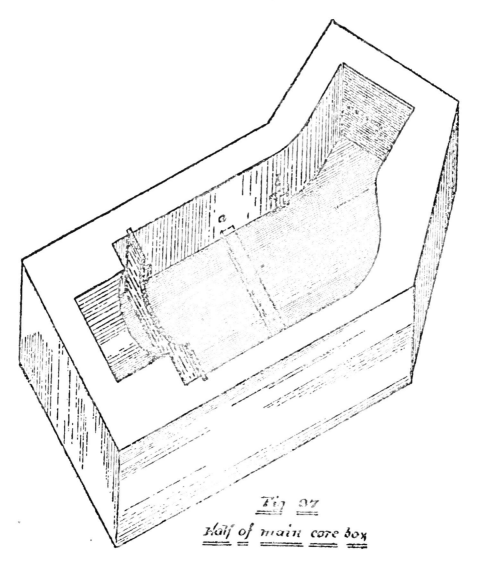

Fig. 97

Half of main core box

cross-section, as shown in Fig. 90. This ring is
then cut into quarters, two of which make the
principal part of the pattern. Next turn up two
pieces (see Fig. 91) in two parts each. These,

when doweled to the quarter circles already
mentioned, make the desired pattern, as shown

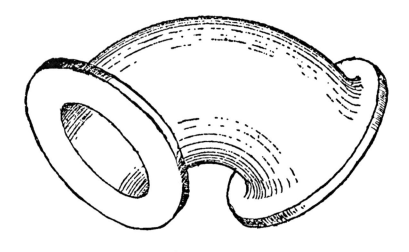

Fig 88
A double flanged steam pipe elbow

in Fig. 92, and it should be painted in the joint,
as shown in Fig. 92. To make a core box for

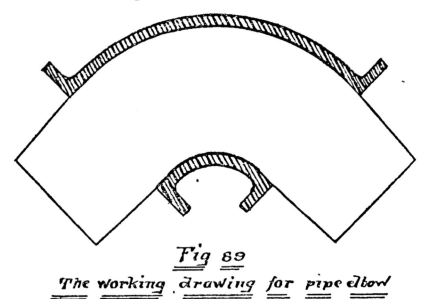

Fig 89
The working drawing for pipe elbow

this pattern, take a piece of stuff of proper
dimensions and into the face turn a semicircular

groove of the radius desired. Cut this plank in quarters, using one of the parts for the curved

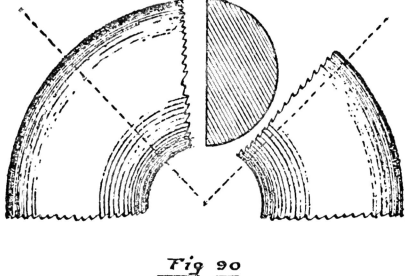

Fig 90

portion of the box, which is finished by gluing on strips in which proper semicircular notches are cut, and with additional strips for closing the ends of the box. This is clearly illustrated in Fig. 93. As the core box is alike at both ends, the core will reverse and glue together; therefore a single box is all that is necessary.

Fig 91

If, however, one end of the elbow should differ from the other, a full box should be made. Now assuming that instead of 4 inches

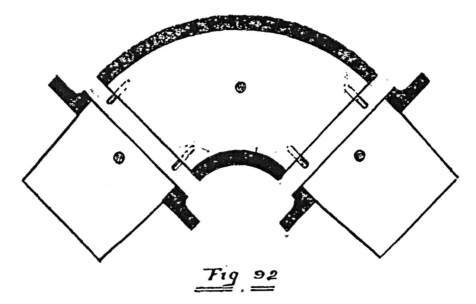

Fig 92

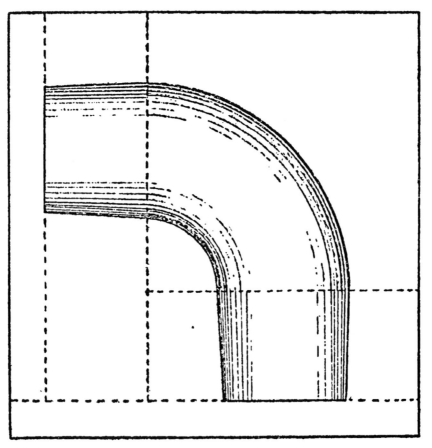

Fig 93

Core box for small sized elbow

this elbow is 4 feet in diameter, then we
have an entirely different proposition to consider, and instead of a piece of lathe work we

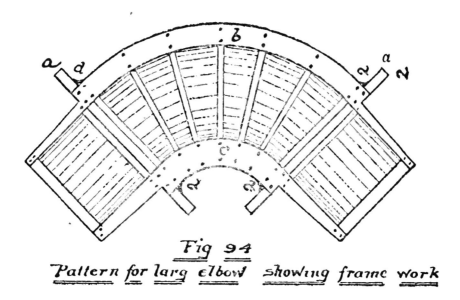

Fig 94

Pattern for larg elbow showing frame work

have a problem in construction which should be
solved in the following manner: Get out the two
circular flanges, *a a*, Fig. 94, which should each be

in two halves and
doweled together.
Next, get out the
pieces *b* and *c*,
and let them into
a suitable gain,
which is cut into

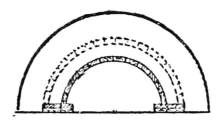

Fig 95

Half pattern for large elbow
showing cross section at flange

the straight side of these flanges. (See Fig. 95.)
Now get out the semicircular ribs for the
body of the pattern, and the ribs and ends

for the core prints. Secure these with large
wood screws and glue to the pieces *b* and *c*,

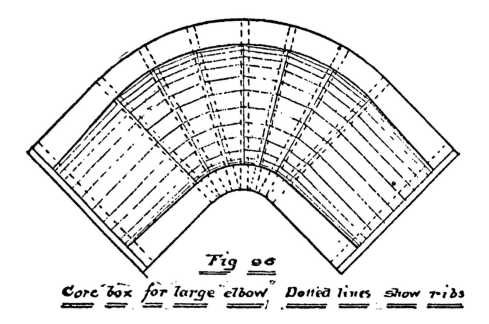

Fig 96

Core box for large elbow. Dotted lines show ribs

as shown in Fig. 94, taking care that a
proper allowance is made for the thickness
of the lagging. Then get out suitable lagging,
the form of which
can be obtained
from the cross-
sectional working
drawing, Fig. 95.
Now cut this lag-
ging to such lengths

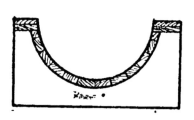

Fig 97

Cross section through core box

as the nature of the work may require, and
secure it in place with glue and screws or
long finish nails, driving all nail heads far

enough below the surface to allow truing up.
Then go carefully over the work with sharp

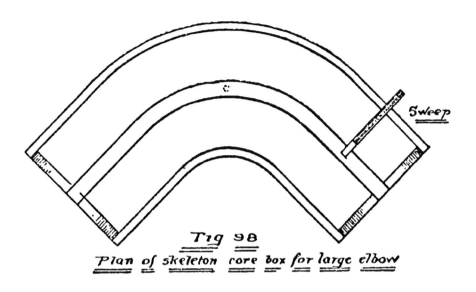

Fig 98
Plan of skeleton core box for large elbow

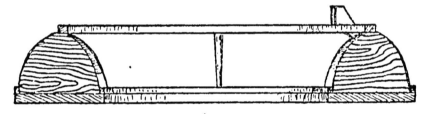

Fig 99
Elevation of skeleton core box for large elbow

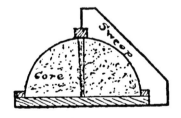

Fig 100
Cross section through core, corebox & sweep.

paring tools, planes, etc., until no bumps
appear when rubbing the hand endways along

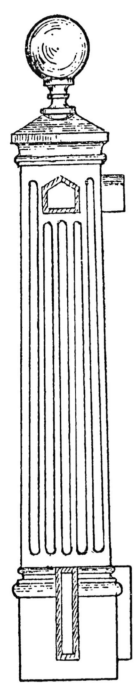

Fig 101

the pattern. Lastly, put a leather fillet[1] at *d* and finish with shellac in the ordinary manner. The making of a core box for this elbow is very similar to the making of the pattern itself, except that the design is reversed; the operation being shown in Figs. 96 and 97. This core can be swept in a skeleton box similar to the skeleton core boxes already described, excepting that from the curved form of the core it is necessary to so design the core box that the sweep may be moved from end to end of the work instead of around it. Such a device is clearly shown in Figs. 98, 99 and 100.

Fig. 101 represents an ordinary fluted cast-iron fence post, which has hollow projections for receiving the ends of the top

---

[1] Leather is now generally used for fillets and is supplied in various sizes by the trade.

and bottom rail of the fence, which is itself hollow.

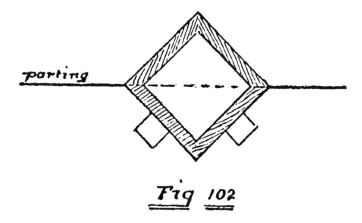

Fig 102

Such a pattern would not draw if divided in the ordinary manner; but the work becomes simple enough when parted as shown in Figs. 102 and 103. The projections for receiving the ends

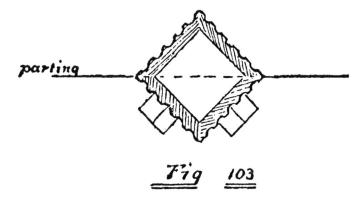

Fig 103

of the rail are left loose from the pattern and are drawn out of the sand after the pattern is lifted, and these, being hollow, leave their own core in the sand.

A suitable core box for Fig. 101 may be made

of the form shown in Fig. 104, especially if any grooves, moulds, etc., are to be shown on the core to correspond with the form of the outside of the post. If a plain square core is all that is required, a core box of the desired form may be made, open at top and bottom, which is laid upon a flat surface filled with prepared sand, flour, etc., and struck off with a straight-edge, as described for the core box as shown in Fig. 25. In this

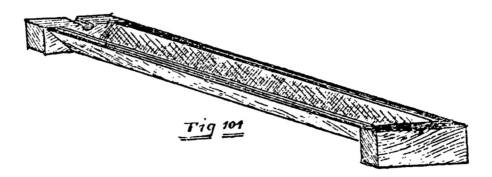

Fig 104

mould such a core would lie with the corner upward.

Having endeavored to treat the subjects of this work in a manner both lucid and exhaustive, not only by the directions simply stated, but also by many illustrations, I feel confident that the careful perusal and study of this volume will be a great aid to the intelligent and ambitious mechanic in his battle for success in life in this particular field of usefulness. It was my intention to have added a chapter, or at least a few pages, to this work, upon the subject of the kinds of wood usually employed in the making of patterns; but as the subject has already been so ably treated by a writer in the July, 1904, number of "Carpentry and Building," I have here reproduced the article in full.

WOOD FOR MAKING PATTERNS

"In a recent discussion of the different varieties of wood adapted to the making of patterns, M. J. Golden, Professor of Applied Mechanics at Purdue University, Lafayette, Ind., brought out some very important points to be considered by the pattern maker, and as the subject is one in which a large class among our readers is interested, we take space to present the following extracts:

"A suitable wood for pattern making must be cheap, of such a nature that it can be shaped or formed easily, have a fine grain and a fair degree of strength. The requisite of cheapness throws out of the list—except for special or restricted use—some woods, such as cherry and mahogany, from which excellent patterns may be made. A study of the microscopic structure of the wood will show why certain classes are not and cannot be suitable for pattern making. For instance, take oak and pine, which are very much alike in cost and the ease with which they may be shaped. Oak, however, is not at all suitable for patterns, while pine, though weaker, is much to be preferred, and is used more than all other woods. Some knowledge of the structure and growth of the two will help us to understand this. Upon examination we find that the pine has a texture that is smooth and even, while the oak has a very great variation in the wood which is formed in the spring of the year, and that which is formed in the summer. The spring growth is open and has many holes that follow the direction of the grain, while the summer wood is dense and hard. In addition, in the oak we find the hard, shell-like plates that form the silver grain comparatively large and numerous; while in pine these plates are hardly distinguishable at all.

"One requisite of a good pattern wood is that it must be of such a nature that the grain can be filled with shellac varnish or some corresponding medium, to protect the pattern from the action of moisture in the moulding sand. It is evident that the wood of the oak will serve this purpose but poorly, and that pine would be much better.

"The wood of the oak is made up practically of two different kinds of elements; one kind is called the vessel. This is shaped like a tube, which may and often does extend the whole length of the tree trunk. The structure of this vessel is much like that of a wire-wound garden hose, except that the ridges are on the inside of the walls of the tube. These ridges serve to stiffen and strengthen the tube. The vessel is for carrying sap from the roots to the branches and leaves. This kind of element forms larger openings, and the vessels have grouped around them elements of the second kind. These are comparatively short in length and much stronger in the walls. The ends of these shorter members overlap and dovetail together; the shorter members are called fibres and serve as a mechanical support to the vessels. The vessels and groups of fibers that surround and stiffen them are together called a bundle.

"There is still another kind of tissue in the oak that forms the silver grain. This is of the same kind that is found in pith, and it occurs in flat plates that connect the outer and inner parts, growing from the heart outward. One of these plates is called the medullary ray and the wood between two of them is a bundle.

"As the tree grows older the tissue in the medullary ray hardens very much, and as it does not change its form during seasoning, it has considerable influence in causing the wood to warp. This greater tendency to warp on the part of the oak is another point against it for the pattern purposes. During the growth of the tree the food matter is taken up by the roots and is carried up to the leaves through the vessels, and there it is brought in contact with the air that it takes in through openings in the surface of the leaves. The sap is then changed into food matter for the tree. The principal portion of the food matter comes from the air, and is carried back with the sap from the leaves to the outer part of the branches and trunk, where it is used in building new wood and other tissue. The medullary rays help to carry food matter to the inner growing parts of the tree.

" Pine wood differs from oak in that it has only one kind of element instead of two. In place of the vessels and fibers there is a kind of element called tracheide that serves the purpose of both. The walls of this tracheide have small openings through them from one to another so that the sap may be carried from the roots to the leaves and back again to the growing tissue. In spring, when the flow of sap is greatest, the elements that are formed by the growing part of the oak are very large and have thin walls, while during the summer the walls are thicker and stronger and the elements correspondingly smaller. The summer wood of the oak is consequently harder and more fine in grain and thus better adapted for pattern making. The difference in the growth in pine at different seasons of the year is much less than in oak, and so, of course, the wood, as a whole, is much more even in grain. When this, and the fact that there is only one kind of element in pine, are taken into consideration, it is evident that the pine is better suited for pattern work than the oak.

"When the pattern maker comes to use these two woods he finds the oak having clearly marked annual rings in which there are, side by side, wood tissue that is very hard and dense from the summer wood, and tissue that is very light and open from the spring growth, so that it is practically impossible to get a surface that will resist the action of moisture in the moulding sand, or even a surface sufficiently smooth to leave a good impression in the mould.

"Then, too, the oak pattern would have a constant tendency to warp because of moisture taken in from the open vessels of the spring wood.

"The pine, on the contrary, has not much difference in the tissue that goes to make up its spring and summer annual rings, these rings being distinguishable more on account of a slight change in color in some parts than on account of the size of the elements. The elements in all parts of the pine are thin and light enough so that the wood is easily shaped, and yet the elements are small enough to make protection of them by varnish an easy matter, on account of the fact that they are easily filled. These peculiarities of structure adapt the pine especially to the needs of the pattern maker, its principal drawback being because of the lightness of its tissue and the ease with which it is bruised."

In conclusion we will remark, that a pattern maker is supposed to be a paragon of order, a thorough mechanic and a gentleman. His tools are of the best quality and in perfect order for turning out the finest quality of work. Every tool is always in place and he knows just where to lay his hands on the desired one. His patterns are all numbered and an accurate record kept of them. He is supposed to know what patterns arc at the foundry, when they went and how many pieces of casting arc required. He is expected to "keep tab" on patterns that leave the shop, and in case such patterns are not returned at the appointed time, he should look after them at once. His shop is clean and pleasant. His material is the best of its kind; the softest and driest pine for ordinary and mahogany for fine work. Hence a job of pattern making is well worth striving after by any person who desires to follow a life devoted to mechanical pursuits.

THE END

TABLE OF CONTENTS

FOUNDRY PRACTICE.

Cast iron washer—Cup-shaped casting—Connecting rod—Fire extinguisher cap—Stake pocket casting. Page.................... 19–2

PATTERN SHOP PRACTICE.

Mechanical drawing—Drafting tools—Location of machinery—Gluing up work. Page. 37–48

TOOLS.

Lathe tools, chisels and gouges—Shrinkage rule—Pattern maker's lathe. Page....... 49–58

MAKING THE PATTERN.

Stake pocket pattern and core box—Flanged cylinder pattern and core box—Cast pipe fitting and core box—Double flanged wheel pattern and core box—Double flanged gear—Brake wheel pattern—Making a gear pattern —Laying out gear teeth—Miter gear pattern —Iron dome pattern and core box—Car seat pattern. Page.................... 59–96

CASTING WITH PART PATTERNS, ETC.

Ribbed plate—Cast gear—Large pulley or flywheel. Page.................... 97–104

SWEEP WORK.

Sweep for bowl or dome—Sweep for smoke box door—Sweep for locomotive cylinder— Mould for fluted column. Page..........105–117

COMPLICATED PATTERNS.

Locomotive chime whistle—Car journal box —Double flanged elbow—Skeleton core for large elbow—Fluted cast iron fence post. Page....................................118–138

WOOD FOR PATTERN MAKING.

Oak—Pine. Page....................139–145

MODERN LOCOMOTIVE ENGINEERING

20th Century Edition

By C. F. SWINGLE, M. E.

THE most modern and practical work published, treating upon the construction and management of modern locomotives, both simple and compound.

The aim of the author in compiling this work was to furnish to locomotive engineers and firemen, in a clear and concise manner, such information as will thoroughly equip them for the responsibilities of their calling. The subject-matter is arranged in such a manner that the fireman just entering upon his apprenticeship may, by beginning with chapter I, learn of his duties as a fireman and then, by closely following the make-up of the book in the succeeding pages, will be able to gain a thorough knowledge of the construction, maintenance and operation of all types of engines.

Breakdown, and what to do in cases of emergency, are given a conspicuous place in the book, including engine running and all its varied details. Particular attention is also paid to the air brake, including all new and improved devices for the safe handling of trains.

The book contains over 600 pages and is beautifully illustrated with line drawings and half-tone engravings. Plain, simple and explicit language is used throughout the book, making it unquestionably the most modern treatise on this subject in print,

Size 5 x 6¾. Pocket-book style. Full seal grain leather, with gold stampings and gold edges. **Price, $3.00**

Sent Postpaid to any Address in the World upon Receipt of Price

FREDERICK J. DRAKE @ CO.

PUBLISHERS

211-213 E. Madison Street   Chicago, Ill.

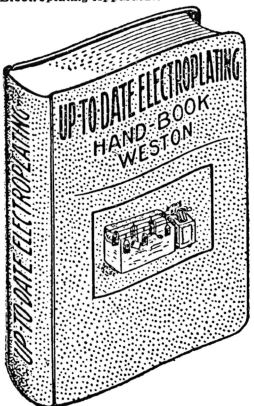

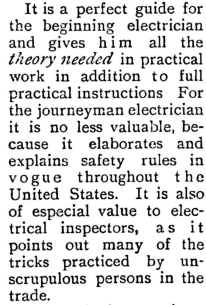

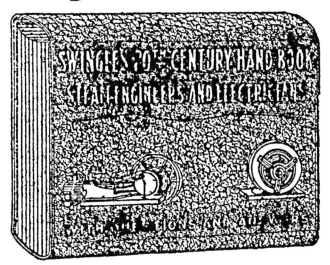

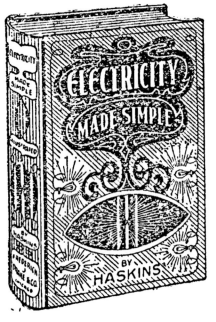

STEEL SQUARE
A TREATISE OF THE PRACTICAL USES OF
By FRED. T. HODGSON, Architect.

New and up-to-date. Published May 1st, 1903. Do not mistake this edition for the one published over 20 years ago.

This is the latest practical work on the Steel Square and its uses published. It is thorough, accurate, clear and easily understood. Confounding terms and phrases have been religiously a v o i d e d w h e r e possible, and everything in the book has been made so plain that a boy twelve years of age, possessing ordinary intelligence, can understand it from beginning to end.

It is an exhaustive work including some very ingenious devices for laying out bevels for rafters, braces and other inclined work; also chapters on the Square as a calculating machine, showing how to measure Solids, Surfaces and Distances—very useful to builders and estimators. Chapters on roofing and how to form them by the aid of the Square. Octagon, Hexagon, Hip and other roofs are shown and explained, and the manner of getting the rafters and jacks given. Chapters on heavy timber framing, showing how the Square is used for laying out Mortises, Tenons, Shoulders, Inclined Work, Angle Corners a n d similar work. The work also contains a large number of diagrams, showing how the Square may be used in finding Bevels, Angles, Stair Treads and bevel cuts for Hip, Valley, Jack and other Rafters, besides methods for laying out Stair Strings, Stair Carriages and Timber Structures generally. Also contains 25 beautiful halftone illustrations of the perspective and floor plans of 25 medium priced houses.

The work abounds with hundreds of fine illustrations and explanatory diagrams which will prove a perfect mine of instruction for the mechanic, young or old.

Two large volumes, 560 pages, nearly 500 illustrations, printed on a superior quality of paper from new large type.

Price, 2 Vols., cloth binding	$2.00
Price, 2 Vols., half-leather binding	3.00
Single Volumes, Part I, cloth	1.00
" " Part I, half-leather	1.50
" " Part II, cloth	1.00
" " Part II, one half-leather	1.50

SEND FOR COMPLETE ILLUSTRATED CATALOGUE FREE

FREDERICK J. DRAKE & CO.
PUBLISHERS OF SELF-EDUCATIONAL BOOKS

211 E. MADISON STREET   CHICAGO

Modern Carpentry
A PRACTICAL MANUAL

FOR CARPENTERS AND WOOD WORKERS GENERALLY

y FRED T. HODGSON, Architect, Editor of the National Builder, Practical Carpentry, Steel Square and Its Uses, etc., etc.

A NEW, complete guide, containing **hundreds of quick methods** for performing work in **carpentry, joining and general wood-work.** Like all of Mr. Hodgson's works, it is written in a simple, every-day style, and does not bewilder the working-man with long mathematical formulas or abstract theories. The illustrations, of which there are many, are explanatory, so that any one who can read plain English will be able to understand them easily and to follow the work in hand without difficulty.

The book contains methods of **laying roofs, rafters, stairs, floors, hoppers, bevels, joining mouldings, mitering, coping, plain hand-railing, circular work, splayed work,** and many other things the carpenter wants to know to help him in his every day vocation. It is the **most complete** and **very latest** work published, being **thorough, practical** and **reliable.** One which no carpenter can afford to be without.

The work is printed from new, large type plates on a superior quality of cream wove paper, durably bound in English cloth.

Price   -   -   -   - $1.00

FREDERICK J. DRAKE & CO.
211-213 E. Madison St., Chicago.